COOL PRIVATE ISLAND RESORTS
THE WORLD'S 101 BEST ISLANDS

EDITED BY FARHAD VLADI

teNeues

FOREWORD

THE SOLITUDE ACHIEVED by being stranded on a small piece of land surrounded by azure waters awakens our inner Robinson Crusoe, vitalising our sense of adventure and bringing us at peace with ourselves. Whether guests choose to visit a luxurious island resort, a fully staffed private villa or even their own private stake of land in splendid isolation, we're trending back towards nature. In a world of urbanisation and constant change, nature serves as one of the few constants we have. With many of the islands scattered across the globe left intact, it's no wonder that we are drawn to these places of calm and repose. Every isle has its own unique character, giving us well-nigh endless locations to discover year after year, without us having to sacrifice comfort and modern technology.

It doesn't take a genius to recognise why millionaires and celebrities have always been drawn to these places. Discretion is top priority for most owners. I remember being contacted by an alleged attorney who spent some time on Frégate Island in the Seychelles. As customary, I checked in to see how things were going, and it turns out the guest was none other than Bill Gates.

What may sound like an extravagant holiday for some actually contributes to the preservation and very existence of these idyllic retreats. Discerning owners know that by allowing guests to stay at their private havens, they are actually safeguarding them from dereliction. The collected rent helps protect and maintain the houses and grounds. And as our mothers taught us whilst growing up, sharing in itself can be a rewarding experience. It always brings a smile to my face when I receive thank you letters from island owners and read the ecstatic guestbook entries from the visitors.

British entrepreneur Sir Richard Branson has been a pioneer in the world of private islands. I was invited to visit his beloved Necker Island in the British Virgin Islands in the '90s. It was here that he asked me to help him transform this into a place for others to enjoy. For the most part, our clients were and continue to be island enthusiasts, so why not also allow short-term visits? Shortly after letting Necker Island for the first time, the Seychelles opened the gates for Frégate and Cousine Islands, and the enchanting Sleepy Cove in Nova Scotia quickly followed suit. At first, I thought that letting would negatively affect the sale of islands. But Richard was right in the end: it has actually perpetuated their sale.

Vladi Private Islands has organised 20,000 trips and sold over 2,000 islands in the past 40 years. I've visited many of them, and seen their transformation. My passion for the world's beautiful atolls, oceanic and lake isles, river islands and peninsulas continues to grow. This is why it came naturally to me to select the 101 best resort islands in the world. With this, I hope you enjoy the literary journey to your favourite island. If you would like your own private piece of paradise, I'd be happy to be of assistance.

EINE REISE AUF eine Insel verheißt uns Menschen eine Zeit im Paradies. Ein Fleckchen Land mitten im Meer stillt die Sehnsucht nach Frieden, in der Einsamkeit findet man Ruhe – wer freiwillig strandet, genießt das Robinson-Dasein. Immer mehr Erholungsuchende wählen ein luxuriöses Inselresort, eine private Inselvilla mit Personal oder ein kleines Seeeiland mit Blockhaus, in dem man sich selbst versorgt. Die Inseln vereinen scheinbar widersprüchliche Reisetrends: Der Urlauber sucht die Natur – doch liebt gehobenen Komfort und moderne Technik. Er sehnt sich nach Stille ebenso wie nach Abwechslung. Nach dem glücklichen Abtauchen in die eine Inselwelt entdeckt man im nächsten Jahr begeistert eine andere, denn jede Insel hat ihren speziellen Charakter. Anstatt Kosten und Verantwortung für das eigene Ferienhaus am stets selben Ort zu tragen, gönnt man sich eine private Oase auf Zeit.

Viele prominente Inselgäste schätzen, dass meist niemand von ihrem Aufenthaltsort erfährt. Diskretion ist den Eigentümern heilig. Ich erinnere mich gern daran, wie sich ein vermeintlicher Rechtsanwalt auf Frégate Island in den Seychellen erholte und ich mich nach seinem Wohlbefinden erkundigte. Der Anwalt freute sich sehr und outete sich als Bill Gates.

Die Sehnsucht nach dem Inselleben tut den privaten Eigentümern gut: Öffnen sie ihr Eiland für Gäste, ist die professionelle Versorgung des Lieblingswohnortes abgesichert. Das Wohnhaus wird stetig gereinigt und gepflegt, Reparaturen sind erledigt und die Grünanlagen kultiviert, das Boot ist gewartet und einsatzbereit. Die Erholung kann mit der Anreise beginnen. Es kann sehr erfüllend sein, das Inselglück zu teilen. So mancher Inseleigentümer berichtete mir von Dankesbriefen und euphorischen Gästebuch-einträgen. Zudem ist der finanzielle Aspekt zu bedenken: Die Mieten sind willkommen zur Deckung der wie bei jeder Immobilie anfallenden Unterhaltskosten.

Der bekannte britische Unternehmer Richard Branson war ein Pionier der Wandlung von Privatinseln in Urlaubsparadiese auf Zeit. Als Herr Branson mich in den 90er Jahren auf seine geliebte Insel Necker Island in den British Virgin Islands einlud, bat er mich, bei der Vermietung seines Urlaubsparadieses mitzuwirken. Immerhin waren und sind unsere zahlreichen Kunden fast durchweg Inselliebhaber. Bald nach der ersten Vermietung Necker Islands eröffnete die Seychellen-Schönheit Frégate Island ihre Pforten als Resort, kurz darauf ihre Nachbarinsel Cousine Island sowie die verwunschene kleine Blockhausinsel Sleepy Cove im kanadischen Nova Scotia. Anfangs dachte ich, wenn ich die Inselvermietung aktiv fördere, würde ich langfristig weniger Inseln verkaufen. Doch Richard sollte Recht behalten: Die Inselvermietung wirkte wie ein Motor für den Inselmarkt und regte etliche Liebhaber an, ein eigenes Eiland zu erwerben. Und die Inseleigentümer schaffen den Spagat: Die einträgliche Vermietung ihres eigenen Eilandes macht einen Aufenthalt auf einer gemieteten Insel zu einer schönen Abwechslung.

Vladi Private Islands hat in 40 Jahren 20 000 Inselreisen vermittelt und 2 000 Eilande verkauft. Viele habe ich immer wieder besucht, habe gesehen, wie sie sich wandeln und gedeihen – wie Familienmitglieder. Meine Liebe zu all den so unterschiedlichen Atollen, Ozean- und Seeinseln, Flussinseln und Halbinseln wächst noch immer. Deshalb fiel es mir nicht schwer, die 101 besten Resort-Inseln ausfindig zu machen. So wünsche ich auch Ihnen viel Freude auf der literarischen Reise zu Ihrem Lieblingseiland. Und wenn der Inselaufenthalt Ihnen später so sehr gefallen hat, dass auch Sie Ihre eigenen vier Strände erwerben möchten – ich helfe Ihnen gerne.

LA SOLITUDE QUE nous découvrons lorsque nous posons le pied sur un petit bout de terre émergé entouré d'eaux azur éveille le Robinson Crusoë qui sommeille en nous, stimule notre goût de l'aventure et nous apaise. Que nos invités choisissent de visiter une île de luxe, une villa entièrement équipée ou même leur propre petit coin de terre isolé, nous avons pris le parti de la nature. Dans un monde d'urbanisation en mutation perpétuelle, la nature est l'un de nos derniers refuges. De nombreuses îles à travers le monde ont su préserver leur authenticité ; notre besoin de calme et de tranquillité nous attire vers elles. Chaque destination est unique et nous propose une myriade de possibilités, année après année, sans devoir sacrifier le confort et la technologie moderne.

Pas besoin de longues études pour comprendre pourquoi millionnaires et célébrités ont toujours été séduits par ces destinations. La discrétion est la priorité de la plupart des propriétaires. Je me souviens avoir été contacté par un présumé avocat ayant séjourné sur Frégate Island, dans les Seychelles. Comme il se doit, j'ai vérifié, pour m'assurer du bon déroulement des choses, et il s'est avéré que l'invité en question n'était autre que Bill Gates.

Ce qui peut sembler extravagant pour les uns contribue en réalité à la protection et à l'existence même des ces retraites idylliques. Les propriétaires avisés savent qu'en permettant à des invités de séjourner dans leurs havres privés, ils les préservent en fait de la déréliction. Les loyers ainsi collectés permettent d'entretenir les logements et les terres. Et comme nous le disaient nos mères, le partage en lui-même est une expérience enrichissante. C'est un plaisir chaque fois renouvelé de recevoir des lettres de remerciement de la part des propriétaires et de lire les commentaires exaltés des visiteurs dans les livres d'or.

Richard Branson, l'entrepreneur britannique, fut un pionnier dans le monde des îles privées. Dans les années 1990, je fus invité à visiter sa chère Necker Island, dans les Îles Vierges britanniques. À cette occasion, il me proposa de l'aider à transformer ce lieu pour en faire profiter les autres. Pour la plupart, nos clients étaient, et restent, de grands amateurs d'îles perdues, alors pourquoi ne pas leur proposer des visites courtes ? Peu après l'ouverture de Necker Island, les Seychelles permirent l'accès aux îles Frégate et Cousine. Sleepy Cove et Nova Scotia suivirent. J'ai d'abord pensé que la location aurait un effet négatif sur la vente des îles. Mais Richard eut finalement raison : elle n'a fait que la favoriser.

Vladi Private Islands a organisé 20 000 séjours et vendu plus de 2 000 îles au cours des 40 dernières années. J'en ai visité de nombreuses et constaté leur transformation. Ma passion pour les atolls, les îles océaniques, lacustres et fluviales, et les péninsules ne cesse de croître. C'est ainsi qu'a naturellement émergé l'idée de ce catalogue des 101 plus belles îles du monde. J'espère que vous apprécierez ce voyage littéraire vers vos destinations préférées. Si vous cherchez un coin de paradis bien à vous, je suis toujours à votre disposition.

Одиночество на маленьком клочке земли, еньком клочке земли, окруженном лазурными водами, пробуждает в нас Робинзона Крузо и страсть к приключениям. Будь то роскошный курортный остров, полностью укомплектованная частная вилла или же частные владения в укромном уголке, мы всегда стремимся вернуться к природе и уединению. В мире урбанизации и постоянных изменений природа является одной из немногих неизменных ценностей. Так как многие острова во всем мире сохранились в девственной чистоте, не удивительно, что нас тянет туда – в тишину и покой. Каждый остров имеет свой собственный уникальный характер, и все они расположены в самых различных местах, где год за годом их можно открывать для себя, не жертвуя при этом комфортом и современными технологиями.

Нетрудно понять, почему эти места всегда притягивали миллионеров и знаменитостей. Конфиденциальность является высшим приоритетом для большинства владельцев. Один раз со мной на связь вышел человек, назвавшийся адвокатом, который провел некоторое время на острове Фрегат Сейшельского архипелага. Как обычно, я проверил информацию и оказалось, что гость был не кто иной, как Билл Гейтс.

То, что может показаться экстравагантным отдыхом для некоторых людей, на самом деле способствует сохранению этих идиллических мест. Предусмотрительные хозяева знают, что, предлагая гостям остановиться в своих частных владениях, они на самом деле сохраняют их от запустения. Собранные средства помогают сохранить дома и земельные участки. Нас с детства учили, что делиться – это хорошо. Я всегда улыбаюсь, когда получаю письма с благодарностью от владельцев островов и вижу восторженные записи посетителей в гостевой книге.

Британский предприниматель Ричард Брэнсон – пионер в мире частных островов. В 90-х годах я был приглашен навестить его любимый остров Некер на Британских Виргинских островах. Именно здесь он меня попросил помочь ему преобразить остров в место, которым смогут наслаждаться другие люди. Большинство наших клиентов всегда были энтузиастами поездок на острова, так почему бы также не позволить им краткосрочные визиты? Вскоре после первой сдачи в аренду острова Некер, Сейшельские острова открыли доступ на острова Фрегат и Кузин, а затем их примеру последовал волшебный остров Слипи Коув («Сонная Бухта») в Новой Шотландии. Сначала я думал, что аренда может отрицательно повлиять на продажу островов. Но Ричард был прав: напротив, аренда островов укрепляет их продажу.

За последние 40 лет компания Vladi Private Islands организовала 20 000 поездок и продала более 2 000 островов. Я побывал на многих из них, и видел их преобразование. Моя страсть к самым красивым коралловым рифам, океанским и озерным островам и полуостровам продолжает расти. В связи с этим, у меня естественно возникла идея выбрать 101 лучший курортный остров в мире. Я надеюсь, вам понравится это литературное путешествие на ваш любимый остров. Если вы хотите свой собственный кусочек рая, я всегда рад оказать помощь.

Safe travels! Gute Reise! Bon voyage ! Желаю вам безопасных путешествий!
Farhad Vladi

CANADA – BRITISH COLUMBIA
24 King Pacific Lodge (p 51)

USA – NEW YORK
19 Cherry Island (p 51)
20 Singer Castle on Dark Island (p 52)
21 Galloo Island (p 56)

USA – CALIFORNIA
22 East Brother Island (p 58)

USA – FLORIDA
23 Melody Key Private Island (p 60)

BELIZE
13 Royal Belize (p 9)
14 Cayo Espanto (p 44)

PANAMA
15 Isla de Coco (p 9)
16 Porcada (p 46)

GRENADA
12 Calivigny Island (p 42)

CHILE
17 Isla Robinson Crusoe (p 9)

CANADA – NOVA SCOTIA
25 Hunt Island (p 62)
26 Mersey River Lodge (p 51)

USA – MAINE
18 Nautilus Island (p 51)

BAHAMAS
1 Musha Cay (p 10)
2 Little Whale Cay (p 14)
3 Bonefish Cay (p 18)
4 Over Yonder Cay (p 20)

TURKS & CAICOS
5 Parrot Cay by COMO (p 22)

BRITISH VIRGIN ISLANDS
6 Guana Island (p 26)
7 Necker Island (p 28)
8 Peter Island Resort & Spa (p 32)

GRENADINES
9 Mustique Island (p 34)
10 Petit St. Vincent (p 38)
11 Canouan Island (p 40)

SWEDEN
92 Dämmans Fyr (p 181)
93 Stora Rullingen (p 194)
94 Island Lodge
   Bergholmen (p 196)

NORWAY
91 Løksøya Island (p 181)

SCOTLAND
86 Isle of Eriska (p 184)
87 Sanda Island (p 186)

IRELAND
84 Fota Island (p 181)
85 Waterford Castle Hotel
   & Golf Resort (p 182)

SPAIN
99 Tagomago (p 204)

GREECE
100 Silver Island Yoga (p 206)

GREAT BRITAIN
88 Tresco Island (p 181)
89 Osea Island (p 188)
90 Spitbank Fort (p 190)

ZANZIBAR
82 &Beyond Mnemba Island Lodge (p 176)

MOZAMBIQUE
83 Vamizi Island (p 178)

TABLE OF CONTENTS

Grenada, Calivigny Island

CARIBBEAN, CENTRAL AMERICA & SOUTH AMERICA

CHILE
ISLA ROBINSON CRUSOE

Go back to where it all began and discover the story of the real Robinson Crusoe.
Der Ort, an dem alles begann … Hier wandelt man auf den Spuren des echten Robinson Crusoe.
Revenez aux origines et découvrez l'histoire du véritable Robinson Crusoë.
Вернитесь туда, где все началось, и откройте для себя историю реального Робинзона Крузо.

PANAMA
ISLA DE COCO

A real-life treasure island – the Treasure of Lima is said to be buried here!
Eine echte Schatzinsel – der sagenhafte Schatz von Lima soll hier vergraben sein!
Une véritable île au trésor – on raconte que le Trésor de Lima y est enfoui !
Остров сокровищ в реальной жизни – говорят, что знаменитые сокровища Лимы зарыты именно здесь!

BELIZE
ROYAL BELIZE

A fully staffed, serene, seven acre private island waits for you with open arms.
Auf dem ruhigen, drei Hektar großen Eiland mit Personal werden Gäste herzlich empfangen.
Les trois hectares de cette île privée vous tendent les bras. Un havre de sérénité à votre disposition.
Полностью укомплектованный, безмятежный частный остров площадью семь акров ждет вас с распростертыми объятиями.

BAHAMAS
MUSHA CAY

With its 150 acres of sparkling, sugar-sand beaches, its crystal clear turquoise waters and its intoxicating tropical environment, isn't it time you did a disappearing act to David Copperfield's Musha Cay? Hidden on the outskirts of the exotic Exumas and surrounded by sandbanks stretching as far as the eye can see, Musha Cay is home to no more than 24 guests at a time – an oasis of tranquillity easily affording guests the space and time they so dearly crave.

60 Hektar glitzernde Pudersandstrände, türkisfarbenes kristallklares Wasser und eine berauschende tropische Natur – ist es nicht Zeit, diesem Zauber zu verfallen und für eine Weile auf David Copperfields Musha Cay zu verschwinden? Verborgen in der Peripherie der exotischen Exumas und umgeben von Sandbänken soweit das Auge reicht, beherbergt Musha Cay maximal 24 Gäste. Eine Oase der Ruhe, die ihren Besuchern Zeit und Raum zur Entfaltung im Überfluss schenkt.

Avec ses 60 hectares de plages étincelantes de sable fin, ses eaux turquoise et cristallines et son décor tropical enivrant, il est temps pour vous de jouer les David Copperfield et de disparaître à Musha Cay. Nichée dans l'archipel des îles Exumas et entourée de bancs de sable infinis, Musha Cay n'abrite pas plus de 24 invités à la fois. Une oasis de tranquillité qui offre à ses visiteurs l'espace et le temps auxquels ils aspirent si ardemment.

Удивительный остров Дэвида Копперфилда – риф Муша площадью 150 акров со сверкающими белыми пляжами, кристально-чистой бирюзовой водой и опьяняющей тропической атмосферой похож на чудесный мираж, где можно укрыться от мира. Скрытый на окраине экзотического района Эксумас и окруженный отмелями, простирающимися за линию горизонта, – это настоящий оазис спокойствия, где гости могут вволю наслаждаться столь желанным свободным временем и пространством. На острове можно разместить не более 24 гостей.

LITTLE WHALE CAY

Set within an exclusive pocket of the Bahamas, Little Whale Cay is the perfect starting point for an international island-hopping adventure. Only 20 minutes from the chic Bahamian capital of Nassau, Little Whale boasts a quaint wedding chapel, a fully protected harbour, a 2,000 foot long landing strip and incredible accommodation facilities to boot. Capable of hosting twelve guests and adorned with natural, captivating décor, the Cuban-style residence exudes an old world charm, yet the indulgent infinity pool adds a touch of luxury.

In einer exklusiven Ecke der Bahamas gelegen, ist Little Whale Cay ein idealer Ausgangspunkt für ein internationales Insel-Hopping-Abenteuer. Nur 20 Minuten von Nassau, der schicken Hauptstadt der Bahamas, entfernt, kann Little Whale stolz eine malerische Hochzeitskapelle, einen geschützten Hafen, eine über 600 Meter lange Landebahn und erstklassige Übernachtungsmöglichkeiten für zwölf Gäste vorweisen. Die Residenz im kubanischen Stil mit üppigem Naturdekor verströmt den Charme vergangener Zeiten. Der Infinity Pool vollendet das Ambiente mit einem Hauch Luxus.

Nichée dans un écrin préservé des Bahamas, Little Whale Cay est le point de départ idéal pour une aventure internationale à travers l'archipel. À seulement 20 minutes de la très chic capitale, Nassau, Little Whale abrite une chapelle pittoresque, un port entièrement protégé, une piste d'atterrissage de 600 mètres, ainsi que de fabuleux moyens d'hébergement. Capable d'accueillir douze invités, dans un décor aussi naturel que fascinant, la résidence de style cubain respire le charme d'un monde perdu, teinté d'une touche de luxe avec sa piscine à débordement.

Входящий в состав Багамского архипелага коралловый риф Литл Уэйл является идеальной отправной точкой для международных приключений на островах. Расположенный всего в 20 минутах от великолепной Багамской столицы Нассау, этот риф может похвастаться причудливой свадебной часовней, полностью защищенной гаванью, а также взлетно-посадочной полосой длиной 2 тыс. футов и потрясающими местами для отдыха. Великолепная резиденция в кубинском стиле с натуральной отделкой, источающая обаяние старого мира, позволяет разместить до 12 гостей, а великолепный панорамный переливной бассейн добавляет ноту роскоши.

BAHAMAS
BONEFISH CAY

Taking its name from both its interesting shape and the amount of bonefish in the region, Bonefish Cay has undergone a dramatic seven year long transformation, turning a once deserted island into a first class getaway home to five large properties capable of hosting a maximum of 14 travellers. Ideal for a get-together or a private party, Bonefish is the perfect destination for guests used to the finer things in life. Small but perfectly formed, no other island comes close to private island perfection.

Ihre markante Form und der Reichtum an Grätenfischen gaben der Insel ihren Namen. Nach sieben Verwandlungsjahren ist Bonefish Cay aus dem Kokon geschlüpft und hat sich von einer verlassenen Insel in ein exklusives Erholungsparadies verwandelt. Fünf großzügige Unterkünfte beherbergen bis zu 14 Gäste. Ideal für ein Treffen oder eine private Feier, ist Bonefish der vollkommene Ort für Genießer der feinen Dinge des Lebens. Klein, aber makellos geformt, kommt keine andere Insel der Perfektion dieser Privatinsel nah.

Baptisée d'après sa forme amusante et l'impressionnante quantité de bonefish qui peuplent ses eaux, Bonefish Cay a bénéficié d'une transformation spectaculaire au cours des sept dernières années. Jadis déserte, l'île accueille aujourd'hui cinq grandes propriétés de première classe, pour 14 bons vivants en mal d'évasion. Parfaite pour une petite fête ou une soirée privée, Bonefish est la destination idéale pour qui sait apprécier les choses agréables de la vie. Petite mais harmonieuse, aucune autre île privée ne saurait rivaliser d'élégance.

Коралловый риф Бонфиш получил свое название благодаря уникальной форме острова и большому количеству рыбы (bonefish) в регионе. За последние семь лет он претерпел сильные изменения, превратившие некогда заброшенный остров в первоклассное место для отдыха, где находятся пять просторных вариантов жилья, способных принять до 14 гостей. Будучи идеальным местом для совместных развлечений, Бонфиш идеально подходит для самых взыскательных гостей. Этот частный остров отличается своим небольшим размером и идеальной формой, выделяясь среди всех других островов.

BAHAMAS
OVER YONDER CAY

The ultimate luxury retreat with renewable resources, Over Yonder Cay is an exclusive island idyll in the heart of the Exumas, shared by no more than 28 guests at a time. The 72-acre island former fishing outpost has been tastefully transformed into a dramatic showplace for stunning architectural design and cutting-edge green energy technology. Set like a rare jewel amongst sapphire seas, Over Yonder Cay is a mosaic of magical moments – an experience that touches the senses.

Ein Luxus-Retreat mit erneuerbaren Energien. Over Yonder Cay ist ein exklusives Elysium im Herzen der Exumas, das höchstens 28 Gäste aufnimmt. Das 29 Hektar große Eiland war einst eine Fischerinsel und präsentiert Besuchern heute eine faszinierende Architektur und moderne grüne Technologie. Dieses Juwel im saphirblauen Wasser verspricht magische Momente – Over Yonder Cay ist ein Erlebnis, das die Sinne berührt.

Avec ses ressources renouvelables, Over Yonder Cay est la retraite ultime, une île de rêve au cœur des Exumas, qui n'accueille jamais plus de 28 invités. Les 29 hectares de cet ancien port de pêche ont été transformés avec goût en un étonnant défi architectural, alimenté par une technologie énergétique d'avant-garde. Entouré d'eaux saphir, ce bijou d'exception est une mosaïque de moments magiques, une expérience qui touche les sens.

Коралловый риф Овер Йандер - это роскошное место для островного отдыха с возобновляемыми ресурсами в центре Эксумас. На острове можно разместить не более 28 гостей. Ранее использовавшийся для рыбной ловли, этот остров площадью 72 акра был со вкусом преобразован в уникальную достопримечательность с потрясающим архитектурным дизайном и самыми современными технологиями использования возобновляемых источников энергии. Редкий драгоценный камень среди сапфировых морей, риф Овер Йандер – это драгоценная мозаика волшебных моментов и незабываемых приключений.

PARROT CAY BY COMO

Indulge in a personalised sensory spa journey on Parrot Cay by paying the world-renowned COMO Shambhala Retreat a visit to soothe the soul and revive the senses. Located close to the soft, sandy beaches and served by a constant gentle breeze, the chic spa rooms here allows guests to relax in style until the ocean air finally lures to further adventure. Body and spirit are nurtured holistically using natural recipes borrowed from the locals as well as with the island's own ocean-inspired inventions.

Parrot Cay entführt seine Gäste auf eine persönliche Reise der Sinne. Ein Aufenthalt im weltweit anerkannten COMO Shambhala Retreat ist Balsam für die Seele und belebt die Sinne. In der Nähe der weichen Sandstrände und verwöhnt von einer sanften Brise können die Gäste in den schicken Spa-Räumen entspannen, bis das Meeresrauschen zu weiteren Abenteuern lockt. Körper und Geist werden dank einheimischen Naturrezepten und vom Ozean inspirierten Kreationen ganzheitlich genährt.

Offrez-vous un voyage sensoriel personnalisé sur Parrot Cay et laissez la célèbre COMO Shambhala Retreat apaiser votre esprit et stimuler votre corps. Situées à proximité des plages de sable fin et caressées par une douce brise, les élégantes salles de spa permettent aux invités de se détendre avec classe, le temps de laisser l'air marin les attirer vers d'autres aventures. Empruntés aux pratiques locales et complétés par des innovations inspirées par l'océan, les soins holistiques prodigués nourriront le corps et l'esprit.

Насладитесь индивидуально подобранными спа-процедурами для полного отдыха и восстановления сил в знаменитом центре COMO Shambhala Retreat на курорте Parrot Cay. Расположенные среди мягких песчаных пляжей с постоянным легким ветерком, роскош-ные кабинеты для спа-процедур позволяют гостям стильно отдохнуть и расслабиться, пока свежий воздух океана не соблазнит их на дальнейшие приключения. Для полного отдыха и восстановления души и тела здесь используются натуральные рецепты, позаимствованные у местных жителей, а также и собственные островные изобретения, вдохновленные природными богатствами океана.

BRITISH VIRGIN ISLANDS
GUANA ISLAND

Laid-back luxury between lush vegetation and stunning wildlife. Choose between relaxing on one of Guana's seven spectacular beaches or explore 850 acres of island spread across the popular trails. Home to magnificent sunsets, pervasive solitude and an oh-so-casual elegance, this incredible island can host a maximum of 32 guests at a time and is sure to make a lasting impression on each and every one of them. Complemented by flocks of colourful Caribbean flamingos, Guana is really a wild getaway, drenched with natural beauty.

Entspannter Luxus zwischen üppiger Vegetation und faszinierender Tierwelt. Besucher können sich an einem von Guanas sieben Traumstränden erholen oder das 343 Hektar große Eiland auf den beliebten Inselpfaden erkunden. Fantastische Sonnenuntergänge, vollkommene Ruhe und lässige Eleganz, 32 Besucher können die Insel genießen und keiner wird sie je vergessen. Karibische Flamingos vervollständigen das paradiesische Bild. Guana bietet Wildnis, Abenteuer und vollkommene Schönheit der Natur.

Un luxe décontracté, entre végétation exubérante et vie sauvage éblouissante. Venez vous détendre sur l'une des sept spectaculaires plages de Guana, ou partez explorer les 343 hectares de l'île sur ses plus belles pistes. Admirez ses merveilleux couchers de soleil, goûtez à son calme et à son élégance discrète. Cette île incroyable peut accueillir un maximum de 32 invités, qui emporteront avec eux un souvenir impérissable. Avec ses volées de flamants des Caraïbes, cet écrin naturel est assurément l'escapade sauvage que vous cherchiez.

Непринужденная роскошь среди пышной растительности и потрясающей дикой природы. Вы можете отдохнуть на одном из семи великолепных пляжей Гуаны или исследовать 850 акров островного пространства, пройдя популярными пешеходными тропами. Здесь вас ждут великолепные закаты, полная уединенность и непринужденная элегантность. На этом невероятном острове можно разместить до 32 гостей и, несомненно, он произведет неизгладимое впечатление на каждого из них. Стаи красочных карибских фламинго дополняют дикую природную красоту этого острова.

BRITISH VIRGIN ISLANDS
NECKER ISLAND

Just one look at this perfect private island is all it takes for the relaxing rhythm of island life to take hold. A favourite amongst royalty, rock stars and Hollywood icons, Necker Island is perhaps the perfect example of the freedom and fun a private island holiday can provide. The incredible Balinese-style villas provide space for 28 guests, generating an allure so exotic and so infectious that it should come with a health warning. Travellers beware – after a stay on Necker, everyday life may never seem the same again.

Ein Blick auf diese vollkommene Privatinsel genügt, um den entspannten Rhythmus des Insellebens anzunehmen. Rockstars, Adlige und Hollywood-Ikonen – sie alle lieben Necker Island. Die Insel verkörpert absolute Freiheit und Spaß wie kaum eine andere. Die wunderbaren Villen im balinesischen Stil können 28 Gäste aufnehmen und haben einen exotischen Zauber, dem sich niemand entziehen kann. Reisende seien gewarnt, nach einem Besuch auf Necker mag der Alltag nie wieder derselbe sein.

Il ne vous faudra pas plus d'un regard pour vous laisser emporter par le rythme apaisant de cette île privée de rêve. Plébiscitée par les rois, les stars du rock et les icônes hollywoodiennes, Necker Island est probablement l'incarnation même de la liberté et de la détente. Les incroyables villas de style balinais jouissent d'un cadre si exotique, si contagieux, qu'il faudrait presque fournir une mise en garde aux 28 invités qu'elles peuvent accueillir. Prenez garde, voyageurs...la vie après Necker Island pourrait ne plus jamais sembler la même.

Одного взгляда на этот прекрасный частный остров достаточно для того, чтобы ощутить расслабляющий ритм островной жизни. Будучи излюбленным местом отдыха членов королевских семей, рок-звезд и голливудских знаменитостей, Некер — это идеальный пример частного острова, где можно свободно веселиться. Потрясающие виллы в балийском стиле позволяют разместить 28 гостей. Обаяние и экзотика острова столь заразительны, что путешественников следовало бы предупреждать о возможном возникновении зависимости! После пребывания на острове Некер вы уже никогда не сможете довольствоваться повседневной жизнью.

BRITISH VIRGIN ISLANDS
PETER ISLAND RESORT & SPA

One of the most romantic island destinations in the Caribbean, the best thing to do whilst enjoying a stay at the Peter Island Resort & Spa is... absolutely nothing. Pack a picnic and enjoy the midday sun with a chilled bottle of wine or simply unwind in the spa whilst enjoying an array of all-encompassing treatments certain to stimulate both body and mind. Using organic products which capture the potent qualities of private island life, Peter Island is a lesson in relaxation.

Eines der romantischsten Inselziele in der Karibik. Nirgendwo ist das Nichtstun süßer als im Peter Island Resort & Spa. Sie können mit Picknickkorb und Champagner auf Eis die Mittagssonne genießen oder im Spa die Seele baumeln lassen, während Sie die vielfältigen Behandlungen, die Wunder für Körper und Seele bewirken, genießen. Die hier verwendeten biologischen Produkte vereinen alle guten Kräfte der Inseln in sich und tragen ihren Teil zur ganzheitlichen Entspannung auf Peter Island bei.

Lorsque vous posez le pied sur l'une des îles les plus romantiques des Caraïbes, la meilleure chose à faire à Peter Island Resort & Spa est...de ne rien faire. Préparez un pique-nique et profitez du soleil avec une bouteille de vin, ou détendez-vous au spa, où vous pourrez goûter aux traitements complets qui stimuleront le corps et l'esprit. Grâce aux produits biologiques qui capturent les puissantes qualités des îles, Peter Island est une leçon de relaxation.

Пребывание на курорте Peter Island Resort & Spa, в одном из самых романтичных мест на Карибах, располагает к полному отдыху и очаровательному безделью. Отправляйтесь на пикник и наслаждайтесь полуденным солнцем за бутылкой охлажденного вина, или просто расслабляйтесь в спа-салоне с помощью комплексных процедур, стимулирующих тело и ум с помощью натуральных островных продуктов. На курорте Peter Island Resort & Spa вы научитесь расслабляться.

Uniquely positioned atop one of Mustique Island's most coveted vantage points, the Opium Villa is an intimate oasis for up to 14 guests. East meets West via Bali-infused architecture and distinguished contemporary décor, with an opulent Oriental atmosphere sure to delight even the most seasoned of travellers. Six discreet members of household staff are always on hand to ensure that every desire is catered for, meaning you're free to enjoy every minute of this irresistible island escape.

Auf einem von Mustique Islands begehrtesten Aussichtspunkten thront die Opium Villa – eine intime Oase für bis zu 14 Gäste. Abend- und Morgenland treffen aufeinander in der balinesisch beeinflussten Architektur und dem feinen, modernen Dekor inmitten eines orientalischen Ambientes, das selbst die erfahrensten Reisenden begeistert. Sechs Angestellte kümmern sich um das Wohl der Gäste und sorgen dafür, dass alle Wünsche erfüllt werden. So können Sie jede Minute auf dieser unwiderstehlichen Insel genießen.

Idéalement placée sur l'un des points de vue les plus convoités de Mustique Island, l'Opium Villa est une oasis intime capable d'accueillir 14 invités. Le mélange des influences venues de l'est et de l'ouest de cet élégant décor balinais ravira les voyageurs les plus expérimentés, qui ne manqueront pas d'apprécier la richesse de cette atmosphère orientale. Les six membres de l'équipe de maison sauront répondre à chacun de vos désirs, avec la plus grande discrétion. Vous serez libre de profiter de chaque minute passé sur cette île irrésistible.

Уникально расположенный на вершине одной из самых завидных смотровых площадок на острове Мюстик, курорт Opium Villa представляет собой уединенный оазис, где можно разместить 14 гостей. Архитектура в балийском стиле и изысканное современное оформление сочетают в себе культурные традиции Востока и Запада, а пышную восточную обстановку, без сомнения, оценят даже самые взыскательные гости. Шесть сотрудников надежного обслуживающего персонала всегда готовы исполнить любые ваши желания, в то время как вы свободно наслаждаетесь каждой минутой этого незабываемого отдыха на острове.

GRENADINES
PETIT ST. VINCENT

Lying well off the tourist track, Petit St. Vincent is a paradise of towering palms and softly rolling hills spread over 113 acres. Located in the heart of the Grenadines, the 22 wonderfully appointed villas on the island are surrounded by two miles of beaches, bay and coves – the perfect backdrop for a spot of island dreaming! Boasting one of the Caribbean's largest coral reefs to boot, the island enjoys an enviable reputation as a unique island paradise where luxury, nature and privacy combine to provide the ultimate getaway experience.

Weit entfernt von den üblichen Touristenpfaden liegt Petit St. Vincent, ein 45 Hektar großes Eiland mit in den Himmel ragenden Palmen und sanften Hügeln. Mitten im Herzen der Grenadinen, mit 22 wundervoll ausgestatteten Villen, umgeben von über drei Kilometer langen Stränden und romantischen Buchten, ist Petit St. Vincent der Inbegriff aller Inselträume! Eines der größten Korallenriffe der Karibik vervollständigt das Paradies, in dem Luxus, Natur und Ruhe für eine vollkommene Auszeit sorgen.

Loin des circuits touristiques, Petit St. Vincent est un paradis de palmiers géants et de douces collines, sur près de 45 hectares. Situées au cœur des Grenadines, les 22 magnifiques villas de l'île sont entourées de trois kilomètres de plages, de baies et de criques...le décor idéal d'un rêve insulaire ! Dotée de l'un des récifs de corail les plus grands des Caraïbes, Petit St. Vincent est un véritable coin de paradis, où le luxe, la nature et la tranquillité se combinent pour vous garantir l'évasion ultime.

Расположенный вдали от туристических маршрутов, Пти-Сент-Винсент – это райский уголок среди высоких пальм и холмов на площади 113 акров. Расположенные в самом сердце Гренадинов, 22 чудесные комфортабельные виллы окружены пляжами, заливами и бухтами, простирающимися вокруг на две мили. Это – остров, где сбываются мечты. Кроме того, остров Пти-Сент-Винсент обладает одним из крупнейших коралловых рифов на Карибах и завидной репутацией уникального райского острова, где роскошь, природа и уединение позволяют получить максимальное удовольствие от отдыха.

GRENADINES
CANOUAN ISLAND

Unspoilt and virtually undiscovered, Canouan Island is one of the Caribbean's up-and-coming luxury destinations. The perfect blend of European luxury and Caribbean casual elegance, the Canouan Resort is an enchanting escape that won't fail to capture your heart. Promising sun, sea and utter seclusion, the island's enviable location places it only a short distance from the Tobago Cays, providing guests with some of the best sailing conditions in the world.

Ursprünglich und nahezu unerforscht ist Canouan Island ein aufsteigender Stern der Karibik. Das Canouan Resort kombiniert europäischen Luxus mit der lässigen Eleganz der Karibik und kreiert damit seinen ganz eigenen Zauber. Sonne, Meer und vollkommene Abgeschiedenheit erwarten Sie auf dieser günstig in der Nähe der Tobago Cays gelegenen Insel – und Segelbedingungen, die zu den besten der Welt gehören.

Préservée et presque sauvage, Canouan Island est l'une des prochaines destinations en vue dans les Caraïbes. Mélange parfait de luxe à l'européenne et d'élégance caribéenne, le Canouan Resort vous offre une évasion enchanteresse dont vous tomberez littéralement amoureux. Soleil, mer et tranquillité, tels sont les atouts de l'île, à quelques encablures seulement des Tobago Cays, véritable paradis des amateurs de voile.

Нетронутый и практически неизвестный, остров Кануан является одним из перспективных и шикарных островов на Карибах. Идеальное сочетание европейской роскоши и карибской непринужденной элегантности делает курорт на Кануане превосходным местом для отпуска, который непременно завоюет ваше сердце. Солнце, море и полное уединение на острове вам обеспечены. Благодаря завидному расположению неподалеку от рифов Тобаго, гости могут воспользоваться лучшими в мире условиями для парусного спорта.

GRENADA
CALIVIGNY ISLAND

Opulent, affluent and exotic – a trip to Calivigny Island is to discover unsurpassed splendour – a luxurious world where the everyday evaporates effortlessly into the clear blue skies above. Standing out from the pack thanks to its exquisite accommodation, Calivigny Island's incredible Beach House can house up to 20 guests. The very epitome of luxury living, there are few villas on earth that are as decadent as this. A sympathetic blend of French colonialism and Balinese beach house chic, this palatial retreat must be seen to be believed.

Opulent, üppig und exotisch – Calivigny Island ist eine prachtvolle Luxuswelt, in der sich der Alltag unmerklich wie eine Wolke im strahlend blauen Himmel auflöst. Das außergewöhnliche Beach House für bis zu 20 Gäste mit seiner exquisiten Ausstattung hebt die Insel von allen anderen ab. Es gibt nur wenige Villen auf der Welt, die diesem Inbegriff des Luxuslebens gleichkommen. Die harmonische Mischung aus französischem Kolonialstil und balinesischem Beach-House-Schick muss man selbst sehen, um seinen Augen zu trauen.

Somptueuse, prospère et exotique...voyagez à Calivigny Island et découvrez une splendeur à nulle autre pareille. Un monde luxuriant, où le quotidien se dissipe aussi facilement qu'un nuage dans son ciel bleu azur. Loin devant la concurrence grâce à ses exquises installations, le Beach House de l'île peut accueillir jusqu'à 20 invités. Véritable parangon du luxe, peu de villas peuvent s'enorgueillir d'un tel faste. Délicieux mélange de colonialisme à la française et de chic balinais, cette retraite princière est un rêve éveillé.

Поездка на роскошный экзотический остров Каливиньи откроет вам непревзойденное великолепие, где повседневность легко растворяется в чистом голубом небе. Островной дом на пляже отличается прекрасным расположением и позволяет разместить до 20 гостей. Это настоящее воплощение роскоши, и лишь несколько вилл во всем мире могут похвастаться таким уровнем комфорта и элегантности. Этот роскошный особняк, сочетающий в себе стиль французского колониализма и балийского пляжного дома, превосходит самые умопомрачительные фантазии.

CAYO ESPANTO

Designed for discriminating guests who demand the best the world has to offer, Belize's Cayo Espanto is a world-class, five-star private island paradise located on the cusp of the world's second largest barrier reef system. From the comfort of the luxuriously appointed villas, guests will enjoy enchanting evenings filled with Caribbean warmth. Home to only 18 guests at a time, Cayo Espanto elevates the private island experience to a higher plane.

Gehört zur Crème de la Crème der Luxusziele dieser Welt. Belizes Cayo Espanto ist ein privates Fünf-Sterne-Inselparadies an der Spitze des zweitgrößten Barrier Reefs der Welt. Im Komfort der luxuriös ausgestatteten Villen können Gäste den Zauber der warmen Karibikabende genießen. Jeweils 18 Besucher kommen in den Genuss von Cayo Espanto – ein wahrhaft exklusives Erlebnis.

Aménagée pour les inconditionnels du bon goût désireux de bénéficier de ce que le monde à de mieux à offrir, Cayo Espanto au Bélize est une île privée cinq étoiles de réputation internationale, un paradis situé à la pointe de la deuxième plus grand barrière de corail au monde. Confortablement installés dans leurs luxueuses villas, les invités pourront profiter de délicieuses soirées, dans la chaleur des Caraïbes. Capable d'accueillir 18 visiteurs à la fois, Cayo Espanto fait passer l'île privée à un tout autre niveau.

Курорт Кайо Эспанто в Белизе специально создан для самых разборчивых гостей, требующих лучшего, что предлагается в мире. Это пятизвездочный частный остров мирового класса, расположенный на пороге второй в мире по величине системы барьерных рифов. В обстановке полного комфорта роскошных вилл гости могут наслаждаться пленительными вечерами, наполненными Карибским теплом. На курорте можно разместить до 18 гостей. На курорте Кайо Эспанто вы сможете по-новому открыть для себя значение отдыха на частном острове.

PANAMA
PORCADA

Just off Panama's Pacific coast, Porcada is a virgin island escape with modest accommodation for up to ten guests. Located between meandering waters and cool coconut groves, live life like the gauchos and try your hand at rounding up the island's 400 cattle, or enjoy the feeling of the wind in your hair whilst riding on horseback across sweeping golden sands. Truly a place to get together and escape the everyday, Porcada puts an emphasis on the simpler things in life. No other island offers a greater sense of freedom.

Die Isla Porcada an Panamas Pazifikküste ist ein unberührter Garten Eden mit komfortablen Unterkünften für bis zu zehn Gäste. Zwischen schattigen Kokospalmenhainen und sich schlängelnden Wassern kann man zum Gaucho werden und die 400 Rinder der Insel zusammentreiben oder sich einfach den Wind um die Nase wehen lassen, während man über goldenen Sand reitet. Ein Ort, um zu sich zu finden und dem Alltag zu entfliehen. Porcada erinnert an die einfachen Freuden des Lebens und keine andere Insel schenkt ein stärkeres Freiheitsgefühl.

À quelques encablures de la côte Pacifique du Panama, l'île vierge de Porcada accueille jusqu'à dix invités, loin du tumulte du continent. Entouré de rivières sinueuses et de cocoteraies, jouez les gauchos et amusez-vous à rassembler les 400 têtes de bétail de l'île, ou laissez simplement vos cheveux voler au vent tandis que vous chevauchez sur les longues plages de sable doré. Isla Porcada s'attache aux choses simples de la vie, le lieu idéal pour se retrouver et échapper au quotidien. Aucune île n'offre un tel sentiment de liberté.

Недалеко от Тихоокеанского побережья Панамы находится девственный остров Поркада, где могут разместиться для скромного отдыха до десяти гостей. Здесь, среди волн и кокосовых рощ, вы можете почувствовать себя настоящими гаучо и попробовать собрать 400 голов скота, проживающего на острове, или насладиться ветром в волосах, катаясь на лошадях по раскинувшимся золотым пескам. Действительно – это место, где можно собраться вместе и скрыться от повседневной рутины. На острове Поркада вы научитесь ценить простые радости жизни и сможете ощутить ни с чем не сравнимое чувство свободы.

NORTH AMERICA

USA – MAINE
NAUTILUS ISLAND

A historical refuge located within Penobscot Bay – a favourite amongst sailors.
Ein historischer Rückzugsort in der Penobscot Bay – ein Favorit der Segler.
Refuge historique situé à Penobscot Bay, elle est la favorite des marins.
Историческое убежище, расположенное в заливе Пенобскот, – излюбленное
место моряков.

CANADA – NOVA SCOTIA
MERSEY RIVER LODGE

Incredible views of the river can be enjoyed from this pristine island-like property.
Die Lodge am Flussufer inmitten ursprünglicher Natur bietet herrliche Ausblicke
auf den Mersey River.
Découvrez cette propriété insulaire immaculée et profitez de sa vue imprenable sur la rivière.
На этом тихом курорте с нетронутой природой можно любоваться невероятными
речными пейзажами.

CANADA – BRITISH COLUMBIA
KING PACIFIC LODGE

An unsurpassed eco-adventure; this is a fabulous floating lodge like no other.
Die einzigartige schwimmende Lodge ist ein besonderes Erlebnis für Naturliebhaber.
Une éco-aventure fantastique ; une cabane flottante fabuleuse à nulle autre pareille.
Непревзойденное экологическое приключение; это потрясающее, уникальное
жилье на воде.

USA – NEW YORK
CHERRY ISLAND

A great escape that encapsulates the charm of the Thousand Islands' golden era.
Ein malerischer Ort, hier spürt man den Charme der goldenen Ära der Thousand Islands.
La grande aventure, un condensé de l'âge d'or de l'archipel des Mille-Îles.
Удивительное путешествие, позволяющее ощутить очарование золотой эры
Тысячи Островов.

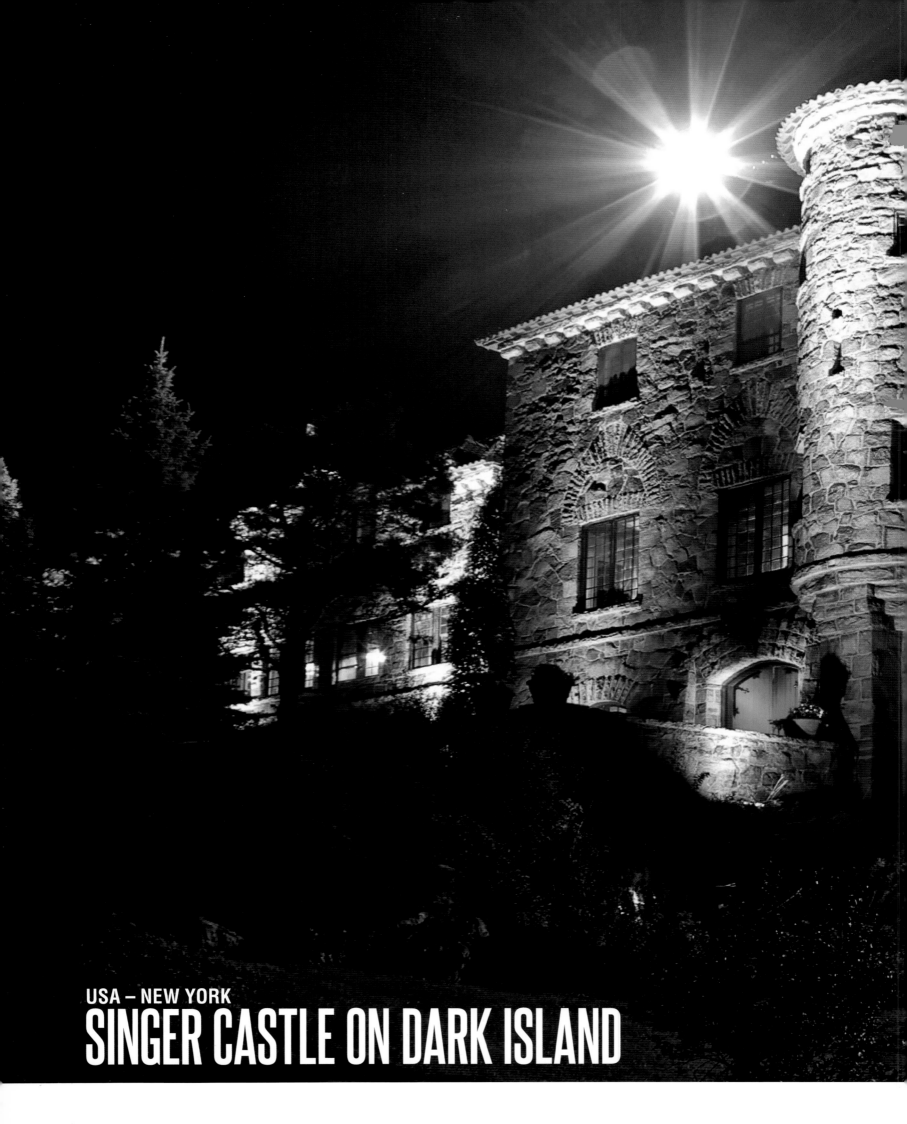

SINGER CASTLE ON DARK ISLAND

Of the 1,864 islands scattered across the 50 miles of the St. Lawrence River, one island in particular stands head and shoulders above the rest. Straddling an international border, the sun rises in the US and sets in Canada on Dark Island. Home to the magnificent Singer Castle, the jewel in the crown of the 1000 Islands chain has attracted attention for over 100 years. The castle can be used as a location for weddings, anniversary celebrations or even a family vacation.

Von den 1 864 Inseln, die über 80 Kilometer im Sankt-Lorenz-Strom verstreut liegen, hebt sich eine besonders von den anderen ab. Mitten im internationalen Grenzgebiet gelegen, geht die Sonne auf Dark Island in den USA auf und in Kanada unter. Als Heimat des sagenhaften Singer Castles, zieht dieses Juwel der 1000 Islands seit über 100 Jahren Besucher in seinen Bann. Das Schloss kann für Hochzeiten, Geburtstagsfeiern oder sogar den Familienurlaub gebucht werden.

Des 1 864 îles éparpillées sur les 80 kilomètres du St. Laurent, celle-ci se démarque de façon originale. À cheval sur une frontière internationale, Dark Island voit le soleil se lever aux États-Unis et se coucher au Canada. Elle abrite le magnifique Singer Castle, véritable bijou de la chaîne des Mille-Îles, qui fascine depuis plus d'un siècle. Le château pourra ainsi accueillir mariages, célébrations ou réunions de famille.

Из 1864 островов, разбросанных на протяжении 50 миль реки Сен-Лоуренс, выделяется один остров, который стоит на голову выше остальных. На Дарк-Айленд проходит международная граница, и солнце встает в США, а садится в Канаде. Здесь же находится великолепный замок Зингер. Этот остров — жемчужина в цепи 1000 островов и привлекает к себе внимание уже более 100 лет. Замок может использоваться для проведения свадеб, юбилеев или даже семейного отдыха.

GALLOO ISLAND

Located towards the eastern side of Lake Ontario and only a short journey away from Upstate New York, Galloo Island is a graceful 2,000 acres of rambling meadows, home to herds of deer and picturesque panoramas of the New England countryside. With accommodation options for twelve guests, Galloo is an obvious choice for nature lovers. Indeed, the island's series of spectacular cliffs, coves and sandy beaches are simply teaming with wildlife, including foxes, beavers, raccoons and a whole an array of avian life forms.

Am westlichen Rand des Ontariosees gelegen und nur eine kurze Reise vom Norden des Staates New York entfernt, hat Galloo Island über 800 Hektar sanfte Wiesen mit Wildbestand und malerische Panoramen der Landschaft New Englands zu bieten. Mit Unterkünften für bis zu zwölf Gäste ist Galloo ein Paradies für Naturliebhaber. Die spektakulären Riffe, Buchten und Sandstrände der Insel beheimaten zahlreiche Tierarten, darunter Füchse, Biber, Waschbären und eine große Vielfalt an Vögeln.

Située sur la rive est du Lac Ontario, non loin d'Upstate New York, Galloo Island offre 800 hectares de gracieuses prairies, parcourues par des hardes de cerfs, dans la campagne spectaculaire de la Nouvelle Angleterre. Capable d'accueillir douze invités, Galloo s'adresse tout particulièrement aux amoureux de la nature. Ses falaises à couper le souffle, ses criques et ses plages de sable regorgent de vie...renards, castors, ratons laveurs et une myriade d'oiseaux.

Изящный Остров Галлу расположен на восточной стороне озера Онтарио и всего в нескольких минутах езды от северной части штата Нью-Йорк. Его площадь в 2000 акров покрыта чудесными лугами, где пасутся стада оленей, и где можно наслаждаться живописными сельскими панорамами Новой Англии. На острове имеются условия для размещения 12 гостей. Галлу – это идеальный выбор для любителей природы, ведь здесь имеются потрясающие скалы, бухты и песчаные дикие пляжи, где живут лисы,

USA – CALIFORNIA
EAST BROTHER ISLAND

Whisking past the ruins of long-abandoned sardine canneries and the remains of the West Coast's last whaling station, the ten-minute boat ride from the Californian mainland to East Brother Island is truly a trip back in time. Dominated by a grand lighthouse and by the silhouette of San Francisco on the horizon, guests of this quaint island will be housed within one of the four bedrooms which make up the old lighthouse keeper's quarters. Boasting the grace and charm of yesteryear, there's no place quite like East Brother Island.

Vorbei an den Ruinen längst verlassener Sardinenfabriken und den Überresten der letzten Walstation der Westküste, ist die zehnminütige Boots-tour vom kalifornischen Festland nach East Brother Island eine Reise in die Vergangenheit. Der eindrucksvolle Leuchtturm und die Silhouette San Franciscos am Horizont sind die Markenzeichen der malerischen Insel. Besucher logieren in den vier Schlafzimmern der einstigen Leuchtturm-wächterwohnung. Liebreiz und Charme vergangener Zeiten machen East Brother Island zu einem einzigartigen Erlebnis.

À travers les ruines des anciennes conserveries de sardine et les vestiges de la dernière station de pêche à la baleine de la côte ouest, la traversée de dix minutes depuis le continent vers East Brother Island est un véritable voyage vers le passé. Entre le grand phare et la silhouette de San Francisco à l'horizon, les invités de cette île au charme désuet seront logés dans l'une des quatre chambres des anciens quartiers du gardien de phare. Redécouvrez la magie d'autrefois dans le cadre unique d'East Brother Island.

Быстро уносясь мимо развалин давно заброшенных рыбных консервных заводов и остатков последней китобойной станции западного побережья, за десять минут, отплыв на лодке от калифорнийского берега на остров Норт-Бразер, вы совершаете настоящее путешествие в прошлое. Гости этого необычного острова с огромным маяком и силуэтом Сан-Франциско на горизонте могут переночевать в одной из четырех спален старинного дома смотрителя маяка. Уникальной особенностью острова Норт-Бразер является особое изящество и шарм прошлого.

MELODY KEY PRIVATE ISLAND

An oasis of peace within the popular Florida Keys region, Melody Key Private Island truly stands out from the crowd, thanks to its relaxed atmosphere and its commitment to environmental concerns. With solar panels in place to really make the most of Florida's famous golden rays, guests can experience castaway chic without the carbon footprint. The spacious, three-bedroom, three-storey timber home boasts all the modern conveniences you could possibly need, whereas the master bedroom provides a welcome touch of luxury in the form of a gigantic Jacuzzi.

Eine Oase der Ruhe inmitten der beliebten Florida-Keys-Region. Die friedvolle Atmosphäre und das Umweltengagement machen Melody Island zu etwas ganz Besonderem. Dank der Solaranlagen, die Floridas goldene Sonne einfangen, können Besucher die vollkommene Ruhe in schickem Ambiente und in Harmonie mit der Umwelt auskosten. Das großzügige dreistöckige Holzhaus mit drei Schlafzimmern ist mit allem Komfort ausgestattet. Das Hauptschlafzimmer verführt mit einem Hauch Luxus in Form eines gigantischen Jacuzzis.

Véritable havre de paix niché dans la région des Florida Keys, Melody Key Private Island ne ressemble à aucune autre, grâce à une atmosphère de détente et de respect de l'environnement. Dotée de panneaux solaires destinés à exploiter le soleil de Floride, les invités pourront jouir du chic de la solitude, sans empreinte carbone. Les spacieuses résidences en bois de trois chambres sur trois niveaux vous offriront tout le confort moderne dont vous pourriez avoir besoin. La suite parentale propose quant à elle une touche supplémentaire de luxe avec son jacuzzi géant.

Оазис спокойствия в популярном регионе Флорида-Кис, частный остров Мелоди-Ки, отличается своей расслабляющей атмосферой и заботливым отношением к окружающей среде. Солнечные батареи позволяют максимально эффективно использовать знаменитые золотые лучи Флориды. Гости могут наслаждаться полным комфортом и роскошью, не оставляя углеродного следа в атмосфере планеты. Просторный трехэтажный бревенчатый дом с тремя спальнями оборудован всеми самыми современными удобствами, а в главной спальне находится великолепная гигантская ванна-джакузи.

CANADA – NOVA SCOTIA
HUNT ISLAND

Deep in the heart of Nova Scotia, overlooking the vast Ponhook Lake, is the enchanting Hunt Island. Promising fun for the whole family, the six-man log cabin is the perfect place to experience an explosion of colours during Nova Scotia's famous Indian Summer or to take a dip in the warm waters of Ponhook. From burnt orange maple trees to beaming blue skies and the soft glow of the lake itself, Hunt Island is a veritable explosion of colour – a spectacle of nature that is guaranteed to take your breath away.

Tief im Herzen von Nova Scotia und mitten im riesigen Ponhook Lake liegt die bezaubernde Insel Hunt Island. Eine Blockhütte für sechs Personen verspricht Spaß für die ganze Familie und ist der perfekte Ort, um den berühmten Indian Summer in Novia Scotia mit seinem unvergleichlichen Farbspiel zu erleben oder im warmen Wasser des Ponhooks zu schwimmen. Vom kräftigen Orange der Ahornbäume über das tiefe Blau des Himmels bis zum sanft schimmernden Wasser des Sees ist Hunt Island ein wahres Farbfeuerwerk und atemberaubendes Naturereignis.

Au cœur de la Nouvelle-Écosse, surplombant l'immense Ponhook Lake, se trouve la merveilleuse Hunt Island. Terrain de jeu de toute la famille, la cabane de six personnes est l'endroit idéal pour profiter de l'explosion de couleurs de l'été indien écossais ou piquer une tête dans les eaux tièdes de Ponhook. De l'orange profond des érables au ciel azur qui se reflète dans le scintille-ment du lac, Hunt Island ravira vos sens. Un spectacle naturel époustouflant auquel vous ne resterez pas insensible.

Глубоко в сердце Новой Шотландии, с видом на огромное озеро Понхук, расположен феерический остров Хант. Бревенчатый дом для шести человек – идеальное место для веселого времяпрепровождения всей семьи. Здесь можно насладиться богатой палитрой красок во время знаменитого бабьего лета в Новой Шотландии и искупаться в теплых водах озера Понхук. От ярких кленовых листьев до сияющих голубых небес и мягкого света озерных вод, остров Хант – это настоящее буйство красок, от которого, без сомнения, у вас захватит дыхание.

FIJI
VATULELE ISLAND RESORT

A cultural melting pot where travellers and native Fijians merge as one.
Reisende und Einheimische vermischen sich in einem bunten Karneval der Kulturen.
Creuset culturel où voyageurs et fidjiens se confondent.
«Плавильный котел», где смешиваются культурные традиции приезжих и местных жителей.

SOUTH PACIFIC

FIJI
TURTLE ISLAND

The long-established Turtle Island is one of Fiji's most famous getaways.
Schon lange ist Turtle Island eines der beliebtesten Ziele auf den Fidschis.
La célèbre Turtle Island est l'une des plus renommées des Fidji.
Давно признанный Черепаший остров — один из самых знаменитых уголков для отдыха на Фиджи.

FIJI
LOMANI ISLAND

Fall head over heels with Lomani – the perfect island for young romantics.
Lomani ist Liebe auf den ersten Blick – die perfekte Insel für frisch Verliebte.
Tombez sous le charme de Lomani, l'île de rêve pour jeunes romantiques.
Летите кувырком, влюбляйтесь на Ломани – это идеальный остров для юных романтиков.

TONGA
MOUNU ISLAND

Enjoy traditional Tongan hospitality on an intimate island sure to make you smile.
Die tongaische Gastfreundschaft auf dem charmanten Eiland zaubert ein Lächeln ins Gesicht.
Découvrez l'hospitalité des Tonga, sur une île amicale et souriante.
Наслаждайтесь традиционным гостеприимством Тонги – этот чудесный остров, без сомнения, вызовет у вас улыбку.

PAPUA NEW GUINEA
LISSENUNG ISLAND RESORT

The Pacific's premiere diving destination; the reefs here certainly don't disappoint.
Bester Tauchspot im Pazifik; die Riffe hier sind legendär.
Le bijou du Pacifique pour amoureux de la plongée. Les récifs ne vous décevront pas.
Лучшее место для ныряния во всем Тихом океане; рифы здесь, безусловно, не разочаруют!

FRENCH POLYNESIA
MOTU TANÉ

A room with a view, perfectly positioned across the channel from beautiful Bora Bora.
Ein Zimmer mit Ausblick – auf der anderen Seite des Kanals liegt Inselschönheit Bora Bora.
Une chambre avec vue sur le lagon, face à Bora Bora.
Комната с видом из окна идеально расположена через канал от прекрасного острова Бора-Бора.

FRENCH POLYNESIA
MOTU TETA

Uniquely special; unspoilt by tourism. Discover the South Pacific as it once was…
Eine einzigartige Perle; vom Tourismus unberührt. Der Südpazifik, wie er einmal war…
Unique et spéciale, protégée du tourisme. Découvrez le Pacifique Sud d'autrefois…
Уникальный и неповторимый; истинный и нетронутый туризмом. Откройте для себя Тихоокеанский южный регион таким, каким он однажды был…

Paradise on earth beneath Fijian skies, Laucala Island is a modern day of Garden of Eden – a heady combination of soft, white sands, lush green mountains and picturesque panoramas. Experience the singular silence of the rainforest and witness spectacular scenery come to life whilst whiling away the hours from the confines of one of the 25 luxury bures, some of which are seemingly carved into the craggy cliffs of the island itself. Dream-like in its splendour, Laucala is an all-encompassing experience sure to stimulate mind, body and soul.

Das Paradies auf Erden unter Fidschis Himmel. Laucala Island ist ein moderner Garten Eden, eine berauschende Mischung aus weichem, weißem Sand, sattgrünen Bergen und malerischen Panoramen. Man erlebt die einmalige Stille des Regenwaldes und das Erwachen dieser spektakulären Szenerie, während man in einer der 25 luxuriösen traditionellen Hütten (Buren), die zuweilen direkt in die schroffen Klippen geschnitzt zu sein scheinen, gemächlich die Zeit verstreichen lässt. Von fast unwirklicher Schönheit ist Laucala ein Erlebnis, das Körper, Geist und Seele inspiriert.

Véritable paradis terrestre sous le ciel des Fidji, Laucala est la version contemporaine du jardin d'Eden : un mélange enivrant de plages de sable blanc, de montagnes verdoyantes et de panoramas époustouflants. Plongez dans le silence singulier de la forêt tropicale et regardez s'éveiller une nature hors du commun, paisiblement installé dans l'un des 25 luxueux bures, dont certains semblent creusés directement dans les falaises escarpées. Laucala est une île splendide qui sait stimuler l'esprit, l'âme et le corps.

Остров Лаукала – это настоящий Эдем под небом Фиджи: опьяняющее сочетание мягких белых песков, пышных зеленых гор и живописных видов. Почувствуйте особую тишину тропического леса и станьте свидетелями оживающих на глазах живописных пейзажей. Растворитесь во времени в одной из 25 роскошных бур, некоторые из которых, казалось бы, высечены в крутых скалах острова. Сказочный остров Лаукала – это незабываемые ощущения для ума, тела и души.

FIJI
NAMALE RESORT & SPA

Discover the secrets of the ocean on Namale Island – a diver's retreat par excellence. A unique combination of privacy and exclusivity, each of the Island's 15 traditional bures overlook the majestic Koro Sea, offering Pacific panoramas guaranteed to make your heart skip a beat. Discover the famous Silver Sage spa or explore emerald waters and captivating coral gardens to discover the pinnacle of tropical luxury. A soothing environment far from the madding crowds, Namale is a sanctuary for the senses.

Namale Island birgt die Geheimnisse des Ozeans und ist ein exzellentes Taucherparadies. In einer meisterhaften Mischung aus Abgeschiedenheit und Exklusivität bietet jede der 15 traditionellen Buren einen Ausblick auf das majestätische Koro Meer und damit Pazifikpanoramen, die das Herz höher schlagen lassen. Das berühmte Silver Sage Spa verheißt Entspannung und das smaragdgrüne Wasser mit faszinierenden Korallengärten einen Höhepunkt tropischer Schönheit. Weitab vom Trubel ist Namale Balsam für die Seele.

Découvrez les secrets de l'océan sur l'île de Namale, le paradis des plongeurs. Mélange unique de tranquillité et d'exclusivité, chacun des 15 bures traditionnels surplombe la majestueuse mer de Koro, offrant des panoramas à couper le souffle. Profitez du célèbre spa de Silver Sage ou explorez les eaux émeraude, au milieu des jardins de corail, véritable joyaux tropicaux. Un environnement apaisant, loin des foules exaspérantes...Namale est un sanctuaire pour les sens.

Откройте для себя секреты океана на острове Намале — идеальное место отдыха для ныряльщиков. Каждая из 15-ти традиционных бур на острове представляет собой уникальное сочетание уединенности и полной эксклюзивности, а из окон открываются захватывающие виды на величественное море Коро. А чтобы в полной мере насладиться тропической роскошью Тихого океана, посетите знаменитый спа-салон Silver Sage или погрузитесь в изумрудные воды с чудесными коралловыми садами. Безмятежная и счастливая атмосфера острова Намале вдали от суеты — это настоящий оазис покоя.

ROYAL DAVUI ISLAND RESORT

If you're looking for a romantic, remote island escape which combines elegant tropical design with a casual castaway lifestyle, Fiji's Royal Davui is the perfect island resort for you. A heavenly cocktail of lush greenery, brilliant white sands and endless blue skies, it should come as no surprise that the island has been dubbed the most romantic island hideaway by certain members of the press. Home to 15 of the most private villas in Fiji, this extra special resort certainly won't disappoint.

Für alle, die sich eine romantische Auszeit auf einer abgeschiedenen Insel mit elegantem Tropendesign und lockerem Robinson-Crusoe-Lifestyle wünschen, werden auf Fidschis Royal Davui Träume wahr. Ein himmlischer Cocktail aus üppigem Grün, weißem Glitzersand und endlos blauem Himmel. Es überrascht nicht, dass dieses Eiland als Gipfel der Romantik gilt. 15 Villen, die zu den abgeschiedensten der Fidschis gehören, erwarten die Gäste. Dieses ganz besondere Resort begeistert garantiert.

Si vous cherchez une escapade romantique sur une île isolée mêlant élégance tropicale et cadre décontracté à la Robinson, le Royal Davui des Fidji vous attend. Ce cocktail paradisiaque de verdure, de plages de sable blanc et de ciel bleu ont valu à cette île le surnom de refuge des amoureux. Elle abrite 15 des villas les plus secrètes des Fidji, vous ne serez pas déçu.

Если вы ищете романтическое уединение на далеком острове, в элегантном тропическом стиле и непринужденной обстановке, то курорт на острове Роял Давуи — это идеальный выбор. Не удивительно, что остров Роял Давуи с чудесным сочетанием пышной зелени, сверкающих белых песков и бесконечных синих небес считается самым романтичным островом. Здесь находятся 15 из наиболее

TOBERUA ISLAND RESORT

Located in the Lomaiviti Group, just to the east of Viti Levu, Toberua Island Resort is made up of four soft, sandy acres just waiting to be explored. Home to a maximum of 30 guests at any one time, this fun-filled Fijian escape offers enchanting views of the South Sea as well as several neighbouring islands. With a beauty which extends far beyond what the eye can see, Toberua Island Resort is not so much a holiday destination but a lifestyle.

Toberua Island Resort gehört zur Lomaiviti Inselgruppe und liegt östlich vor Viti Levu. Über zwei Hektar große, samtene Sandstrände warten darauf, erforscht zu werden. Bis zu 30 Gäste können die Insel genießen. Das stimmungsvolle Fidschi-Paradies bietet bezaubernde Ausblicke auf die Südsee und seine Nachbarinseln. Mit einer Schönheit, die alle Sinne anspricht, ist Toberua Island eher Lebensstil als Urlaubziel.

Située dans la Province de Lomaiviti, à l'est de Viti Levu, Toberua Island Resort est composée de deux hectares de sable doux, qui n'attendent que vous. Capable d'accueillir un maximum de 30 invités, cette évasion fidjienne offre des panoramas enchanteurs des mers du sud, ainsi que des îles avoisinantes. Sa beauté se déploie bien au-delà du spectre visible...Toberua Island Resort n'est pas tant une destination de vacances qu'un véritable style de vie.

Расположенный в группе Ломаивити, к востоку от острова Вити-Леву, курорт на острове Тоберуа — это четыре акра мягкого песка, которые ждут ваших следов. Здесь можно в любое время разместить до 30 гостей. Здесь вас ждет увлекательный отдых, прекрасные виды Южного Моря и соседство нескольких островов. Благодаря своей красоте, простирающейся за пределы горизонта, курорт на острове Тоберуа — это не только прекрасное место для отдыха, но особый и неповторимый стиль жизни.

FIJI
WADIGI ISLAND RESORT FIJI

Picture yourself on the perfect private island – swimming in secluded, sun-speckled water, or unwinding on a soft stretch of sand, listening to the soothing sounds of the South Sea. Now imagine not having to share your tropical paradise with a single soul – with the exception of invited guests and your attentive island staff, that is. Offering unforgettable views of the magnificent Mamanuca Islands, Wadigi Island forms a perfect balance of seduction and seclusion – the winning formula for a first-class castaway retreat.

Stellen Sie sich vor, Sie sind auf der vollkommenen Privatinsel und schwimmen im funkelnden Wasser oder entspannen im weichen Sandstrand zum Rauschen der Südsee. Das Beste: Sie müssen Ihr tropisches Paradies mit niemandem teilen, abgesehen von geladenen Gästen und hilfs-bereitem Personal. Mit unvergesslichen Ausblicken auf die herrlichen Mamanuca Islands verkörpert Wadigi Island die perfekte Balance zwischen Verführung und Abgeschiedenheit – das Erfolgsrezept für eine erstklassige Auszeit im Robinson-Crusoe-Stil.

Imaginez-vous sur l'île privée idéale. Vous nagez dans des eaux protégées et scintillantes, vous vous détendez sur un banc de sable fin, au rythme apaisant des vagues. Imaginez à présent que vous ne soyez obligé de partager ce coin de paradis tropical avec personne, à l'exception des invités et du personnel attentionné, évidemment. Avec ses panoramas inoubliables des îles Mamanuca, Wadigi est l'équilibre parfait entre tentation et intimité. Une formule idéale pour une retraite solitaire de première classe.

Представьте себя в полном уединении на прекрасном частном острове, где вы купаетесь в искрящейся на солнце воде или расслабляетесь на мягком песке под тихий шепот волн Южного моря. Теперь представьте себе, в этом тропическом раю, кроме вас, нет ни души – за исключением приглашенных гостей и внимательного персонала. Открывающиеся великолепные виды на острова Мамануга создают чудесное сочетание красоты и уединения на этом курорте мирового класса.

THE WAKAYA CLUB & SPA

Discover the true meaning of peace and tranquillity at the intimate Wakaya Club & Spa. Set on a 2,200-acre private island in Fiji, the adventure begins aboard Wakaya's very own private aircraft, transporting travellers from the everyday to their extraordinary island sanctuary in no time at all. Home to only 28 guests at one time, Wakaya is both exclusive and inclusive, meaning that whether you're looking for relaxation, recreation or an epicurean experience to top all others, this dream-like destination will not disappoint.

Im intimen Wakaya Club & Spa erfährt man die wahre Bedeutung von Ruhe und Frieden. Auf dieser 890 Hektar großen Fidschi-Privatinsel beginnt das Abenteuer schon in Wakayas eigenem Privatflugzeug, das die Reisenden in kürzester Zeit aus ihrem Alltag mitten hinein ins Paradies transportiert. Bis zu 28 Gäste können Wakaya genießen und hier alles finden, was das Herz begehrt. Entspannung, Spaß oder ein epikureisches Erlebnis, das alles andere in den Schatten stellt – eine Trauminsel am Ende aller Wünsche.

Venez découvrir la paix et la tranquillité ultime au Wakaya Club & Spa. Sur une île privée des Fidji de près de 890 hectares, l'aventure commence à bord du jet de Wakaya, qui transporte les voyageurs de leur quotidien à ce sanctuaire extraordinaire en quelques minutes seulement. Capable d'accueillir 28 invités à la fois, l'île s'ouvre et se protège. Que vous cherchiez détente, loisirs ou expérience épicurienne, cette destination de rêve ne vous décevra pas.

Откройте для себя истинный смысл безмятежности и покоя на уединенном курорте Wakaya Club & Spa, расположенного на 2200 акрах частного острова архипелага Фиджи. Приключение начинается с перелета на частном самолете, который перенесет вас из повседневной жизни на сказочный островной курорт в одно мгновение ока. Курорт Wakaya Club & Spa, где можно разместить не более 28 гостей, является одновременно эксклюзивным и инклюзивным – ищете ли вы спокойный уединенный отдых или незабываемые развлечения, он не разочарует вас!

TONGA
FAFA ISLAND RESORT

Surrounded by the pristine waters of the South Pacific lies an island steeped in tradition. Home to 13 exquisite lodges created according to traditional Tongan construction principles, the fabulous Fafa Island offers the perfect private island refuge for honeymoons, celebrations or simply that extra special holiday you've always dreamed of. Amongst shimmering sands, glistening blue water and lush green vegetation, if you're searching for a natural haven to unwind in, Fafa Island is the destination for you.

Umgeben von den unberührten Gewässern des Südpazifiks liegt diese Insel fest verankert in ihrer Tradition. Mit 13 exquisiten Lodges, gebaut im traditionellen tongaischen Stil, ist Fafa Island ein Traumziel für Flitterwochen, Feiern oder einfach den ganz besonderen Urlaub, den man sich immer erträumt hat. Glitzernder Sand, strahlend blaues Wasser und üppiges Grün machen Fafa Island zum idealen Entspannungsort.

Entourée par les eaux cristallines du Pacifique Sud existe une île imprégnée de tradition. Elle abrite 13 cabanes exquises, créées en accord avec les principes de construction des Tonga. La fabuleuse île de Fafa est le refuge privé idéal pour une lune de miel, une célébration ou les vacances spéciales dont vous avez toujours rêvé. Découvrez les plages chatoyantes, le scintillement des eaux bleues et la végétation verdoyante. Si vous cherchez un havre de paix naturel, Fafa est faite pour vous.

Окруженный кристально-чистыми водами в южной части Тихого океана, находится остров с богатейшими традициями. Здесь имеется 13 изысканных коттеджей, построенных в традиционном стиле Тонги. Сказочный остров Фафа — это идеальное место для того, чтобы провести медовый месяц, отметить памятную дату или просто провести незабываемый отдых, о котором вы всегда мечтали. Если вы хотите как следует отдохнуть и расслабиться, то этот райский уголок среди мерцающих песков, искрящихся лазурных вод и пышной растительности просто создан для вас!

FRENCH POLYNESIA
PRIVATE ISLAND BORA BORA

The simplicity and beauty of Private Island Bora Bora makes this Pacific paradise hard to ignore. Home to a spectacular spa retreat, this incredible island experience is more than enough to put the outside world on hold. Body and spirit are nurtured holistically in a sensual infusion of Polynesian tradition and western luxury, all with the aim of restoring your natural vitality. The breathtaking Bora Bora looms mysteriously on the horizon, further adding to the potent allure of private island life.

Die schlichte Schönheit von Private Island Bora Bora ist etwas Besonderes. Im himmlischen Spa der Insel vergisst man den Alltag. Körper und Geist werden dank der sinnlichen Mischung aus polynesischer Tradition und westlichem Luxus ganzheitlich genährt, alles dient der Stärkung der natürlichen Lebenskraft. Am Horizont ruht mysteriös die atemberaubende Schönheit Bora Bora und verstärkt die ohnehin mächtige Anziehungskraft der Privatinsel.

La simplicité et la beauté de Private Island Bora Bora, au beau milieu du Pacifique, ne laissent pas indifférent. Ce spectaculaire sanctuaire des sens saura vous emporter loin du monde extérieur. Le mélange sensuel de tradition polynésienne et de luxe à l'occidentale est une nourriture holistique pour le corps et l'esprit, qui ranimera votre vitalité naturelle. Époustouflante, Bora Bora flotte mystérieusement sur l'horizon et ajoute une nouvelle touche au tableau intense de cette île privée.

Простоту и красоту тихоокеанского райского острова Бора-Бора с его превосходным спа-курортом невозможно не оценить. Здесь повседневная жизнь сразу отходит на второй план, и вы можете восстановить силы и отдохнуть телом и душой в обстановке, гармонично объединяющей полинезийские традиции и западную роскошь. Невероятный остров Бора-Бора таинственно вырисовывается на горизонте, добавляя привлекательность уединенной жизни на частном острове.

FRENCH POLYNESIA
VAHINE ISLAND RESORT

Suspended between the heavens and the oceans, Vahine Island Resort is a vision of island beauty, where paradise meets perfection and time stands still. Wonderfully remote with only three over-water villas, the atmosphere invites travellers to give in to total relaxation – a world of softly swaying palms, shimmering sand and inviting aromas. Unwind under the soothing hands of skilled therapists and rediscover the relaxing rhythm of long days and leisurely nights.

Zwischen Himmel und Ozean liegt Vahine Island Resort, der Inbegriff einer Trauminsel. Ein vollkommenes Paradies, in dem die Zeit still-steht. Wunderbar abgelegen mit nur drei ins Meer gebauten Villen, lädt die Atmosphäre zur absoluten Entspannung ein – eine Welt aus sich sanft wiegenden Palmen, glitzerndem Sand und betörenden Düften. Die Hände der begabten Therapeuten schenken Erholung. Lange Tage und entspannte Nächte beleben Körper und Geist neu.

Suspendu entre ciel et océan, Vahine Island Resort est une vision féerique, un paradis de perfection où le temps s'arrête. Magnifique-ment isolée, avec seulement trois villas sur pilotis, l'atmosphère du lieu invite les voyageurs à s'abandonner à la détente totale...un monde de palmiers langoureux, de plages scintillantes et d'arômes séduisants. Relaxez-vous sous les mains expertes des thérapeutes et redécouvrez le rythme apaisant de longues journées et de nuits tranquilles.

Курорт на острове Вахин, который, кажется, парит между небесами и океаном, – это образец поистине райской островной красоты, где время застывает. Он чудесно расположен в уединенном месте и включает всего три виллы над водой. Атмосфера острова располагает к полному отдыху среди тихо качающихся пальм, мерцающих песков и чувственных ароматов. Доверьтесь надежным и ласковым рукам опытных терапевтов и вновь откройте для себя размеренный ритм долгих дней и безмятежных ночей.

VANUATU
RATUA PRIVATE ISLAND

Located in the cobalt blue waters of the majestic Vanuatu Archipelago, the sweet-scented island of Ratua is an unspoilt beauty rich with culture and customs. A grand total of 13 200-year-old cottages are dotted across the lush landscape, affording the island authenticity unlike any other. Decorated in a tasteful eclectic style demonstrating a delicate balance between the old and the new, an unparalleled accommodation experience awaits.

Ratua schwimmt im kobaltblauen Wasser des majestätischen Vanuatu Archipels und bietet herrliche Natur, reiche Kultur und Tradition. Insgesamt 13 zweihundert Jahre alte Hütten verschmelzen perfekt mit der üppigen Vegetation und sorgen für ein einmalig authentisches Inselerlebnis. Geschmackvoll dekoriert halten die Hütten gekonnt die empfindliche Balance zwischen Tradition und Moderne – eine wahrhaft außerge-wöhnliche Unterkunft.

Située dans les eaux bleu-cobalt du majestueux archipel de Vanuatu, l'île de Ratua baigne dans le doux parfum d'un environnement préservé, riche de culture et de coutumes. 13 villas vieilles de 200 ans sont parsemées dans un paysage luxuriant et garantissent une authenticité à nulle autre pareille. Décorées avec goût, leur éclectisme assure un équilibre délicat entre tradition et modernisme, pour une expérience hors du commun.

Расположенный в чистейших лазурных водах величественного архипелага Вануату, наполненный ароматами остров Ратуа являет собой нетронутую красоту с богатой культурой и обычаями. Здесь имеется 13 уникальных коттеджей, существующих уже 200 лет и живописно разбросанных среди пышного ландшафта острова. Они со вкусом оформлены в эклектичном стиле, который демонстрирует тонкий баланс между старым и новым. Здесь вас ждет незабываемое впечатление от уникальных условий проживания.

SOLOMON ISLANDS
TAVANIPUPU

The ideal destination for a much-deserved spot of relaxation, the unspoilt white, sandy beaches of the South Pacific's best kept secret are truly unforgettable. A tropical paradise surrounded by a vast, turquoise lagoon, Tavanipupu has a history as colourful as its landscape. Lovingly transformed from a rough diamond into a luxury vacation resort home to 16 magnificent bungalows, Tavanipupu attracts a distinguished clientele from the world over – even the future King and Queen of England have graced its shores!

Ein ideales Ziel, um Körper und Seele zu entspannen. Die unberührten weißen Sandstrände dieses wohlgehüteten Geheimnisses des Südpazifiks sind unvergesslich. Das tropische Paradies Tavanipupu inmitten einer türkisfarbenen Lagune hat eine Geschichte ebenso bunt wie seine Landschaft. Liebevoll aus einem Rohdiamanten in ein luxuriöses Resort geschliffen, warten 16 Bungalows auf Gäste. Tavanipupu lockt eine exklusive Klientel aus aller Welt an – der zukünftige König von England und seine Königin sind schon an dieser Küste gestrandet!

La destination idéale pour un moment de détente bien mérité, sur les plages d'un blanc immaculé...venez découvrir le secret le mieux gardé du Pacifique Sud. Paradis tropical inoubliable entouré d'un vaste lagon turquoise, Tavanipupu jouit d'une histoire aussi colorée que son paysage. De ce diamant à l'état brut a émergé un complexe de luxe abritant 16 magnifiques bungalows. L'île attire une clientèle internationale distinguée... le futur Roi d'Angleterre a même honoré ses côtes de sa présence avec la Princesse !

Идеальное место для столь заслуженного и долгожданного отдыха, нетронутые белые песчаные пляжи южной части Тихого океана поистине незабываемы. Это настоящий тропический рай, окруженный огромной бирюзовой лагуной. История Таванипупу так же красочна, как его ландшафт. Преобразованный из дикого острова в роскошный курорт с 16 великолепными бунгало, Таванипупу привлекает высокопоставленных гостей со всего мира – даже будущие король и королева Англии удостоили посещением его берега!

NEW ZEALAND, AUSTRALIA & ASIA

AUSTRALIA
PUMPKIN ISLAND

A family-friendly island haven for divers, snorkelers and sun-seekers alike.
Eine familienfreundliche Insel – perfekt zum Tauchen, Schnorcheln und Sonnenbaden.
Une île paisible pour la famille, les amateurs de plongée et de ciels bleus.
Чудесный остров для семейного отдыха, настоящий рай для ныряльщиков, любителей подводного плавания и любителей загара.

AUSTRALIA
WILSON ISLAND

White beaches, blue skies and that wonderful laid-back Aussie atmosphere.
Weiße Strände, tiefblauer Himmel und der wunderbar entspannte Lebensstil der Australier.
Plages blanches et ciel bleu dans cette merveilleuse atmosphère décontractée à l'australienne.
Белые пляжи, голубые небеса и чудесная спокойная австралийская атмосфера.

AUSTRALIA
LIZARD ISLAND

The luscious Lizard Island offers the ultimate in indulgence – simply wonderful.
Lizard Island ist der Gipfel an Genuss – einfach himmlisch.
La luxuriante Lizard Island vous offre le plaisir ultime...tout simplement magnifique.
Восхитительный Остров Ящериц открывает своим гостям дверь в мир наслаждений.

THAILAND
SONEVA KIRI RESORT

Traditions, exotic aromas and delicious cuisine combine to inspire the senses.
Traditionen, exotische Aromen und eine exquisite Küche inspirieren die Sinne.
Traditions, arômes exotiques et délices culinaires se mêlent pour éveiller les sens.
Чудесное сочетание традиций, экзотических ароматов и превосходной кухни пробудит чувства даже самых взыскательных гостей.

NEW ZEALAND
FORSYTH ISLAND

From the comfort of your cosy three-bedroom lodge, you will enjoy clean, crisp ocean air and endless Pacific panoramas from soaring peaks stretching far beyond 1,000 feet. With acre upon acre of unspoilt terrain to explore at your own leisure, on Forsyth Island, your only neighbours are of the four-legged variety, leaving you free to explore your island kingdom as you wish. Every day is an adventure in this incredible corner of New Zealand's marvellous Marlborough Sounds.

Von der gemütlichen Lodge mit drei Schlafzimmern aus genießt man die frische Meeresluft und den Blick auf 300 Meter hohe Bergspitzen im Pazifik. Die kilometerweite unberührte Natur teilt man auf Forsyth Island einzig mit vierbeinigen Nachbarn. Sein eigenes Königreich erkunden und jeden Tag neue Abenteuer erleben – all das bietet dieses königliche Fleckchen Erde in Neuseelands malerischen Marlborough Sounds.

Du confort de votre cabane et de ses trois chambres, vous profiterez d'une brise marine aussi pure que vivifiante. Les paysages infinis du Pacifique s'étirent jusqu'aux sommets culminant à plus de 300 mètres. Venez explorer les hectares de terres vierges de Forsyth Island...vos seuls voisins se déplaceront à quatre pattes. Votre royaume n'attend plus que vous. Chaque journée sera une aventure renouvelée, dans cet incroyable paradis des Marlborough Sounds de Nouvelle-Zélande.

Из окна своего уютного коттеджа с тремя спальнями вы можете наслаждаться свежим океанским бризом, панорамой безбрежного Тихого океана и видами горных вершин высотой более 1000 футов. Здесь вы можете исследовать нетронутую местность, а вашими единственными соседями будут разнообразные представители местной фауны. В этом невероятном уголке Мальборо Саундс в Новой Зеландии каждый день — это приключение.

NEW ZEALAND
POHUENUI ISLAND

With an area some eleven times larger than that of the Principality of Monaco, Pohuenui Island counts as one of the world's largest privately owned islands. Somewhat akin to a piece of antipodean Alpine land, the towering summits of this vast island make Pohuenui a natural choice for mountaineers, hikers and other thrill-seekers. Home to a charming cottage and an unpretentious farmhouse, up to 15 people can enjoy rural, rugged adventures, sampling a taste of the real New Zealand as they do so.

Elf Mal größer als das Fürstentum Monaco, ist Pohuenui Island eine der größten Inseln im Privat-besitz. Diese Insel-Alpenlandschaft der Südhalbkugel mit ihren hoch aufragenden Bergspitzen ist ein beliebtes Ziel für Wanderer, Kletterer und Abenteurer. Eine charmante Hütte und eine schlichte Farm bieten 15 Reisenden Unterkunft, die hier die Schönheit Neuseelands ursprünglicher, rauer Landschaft erleben können.

Près de onze fois plus grande que la Principauté de Monaco, Pohuenui Island compte parmi les plus grandes îles privées du monde. Ces montagnes des antipodes attirent alpinistes, randonneurs et amateurs de sensations fortes. Elle abrite une charmante villa, ainsi qu'une modeste ferme, capables d'accueillir jusqu'à 15 invités dans un cadre rural. Venez découvrir cette terre d'aventure rustique et retrouvez la Nouvelle-Zélande originelle.

Остров Похуэнуи в одиннадцать раз превышает территорию княжества Монако и по праву считается одним из крупнейших частных островов мира. Частично напоминая Альпы, горные вершины этого острова делают его особенно привлекательным для альпинистов, пеших туристов и других искателей острых ощущений. На острове имеется очаровательный коттедж и неприхотливый деревенский дом, где можно разместить до 15-ти гостей. Здесь вы получите массу удовольствия от бурных приключений и ощутите реальную жизнь Новой Зеландии.

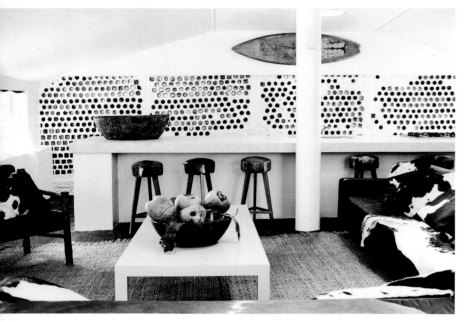

BEDARRA ISLAND VILLA

A haven of understated tropical beauty, Bedarra Island Villa is the perfect destination for divers and sun-seekers alike. Home to a sweeping beach of golden sand and a wonderfully appointed two-bedroom villa reflecting the beauty of its surroundings, this Australian original offers the ultimate in indulgence. Achieving international acclaim for its functional design, the Bedarra Island Villa is perhaps best described as languid relaxation meets comfortable modernism. A must for fashionistas.

In seiner schlichten tropischen Schönheit ist Bedarra Island Villa das perfekte Ziel für Taucher und Sonnenanbeter. Dieses australische Original mit seinem goldenen Strand und einer wundervoll ausgestatteten Villa mit zwei Schlafzimmern verspricht Genuss pur. International anerkannt für ihr funktionales Design, lässt sich die Bedarra Island Villa vielleicht am besten als Mischung aus gekonnter Lässigkeit und komfortabler Modernität beschreiben. Fashionistas kommen voll auf ihre Kosten.

Havre tropical d'une beauté raffinée, Bedarra Island Villa est la destination idéale pour les amateurs de plongée et de plage. Une longue plage de sable d'or s'étire sous le soleil, tandis qu'une magnifique villa meublée de deux chambres vient s'inscrire dans l'harmonie du lieu. Venez goûter aux plaisirs de cette résidence australienne originale. Reconnue internationalement pour son design fonctionnel, Bedarra Island Villa est un savant mélange de détente langoureuse et de confort moderne. Un must pour les fashionistas.

Вилла на австралийском острове Бедарра среди ярких тропических пейзажей – это идеальное место отдыха для ныряльщиков и любителей загара. Изумительный пляж с золотым песком и чудесно оформленная вилла с двумя спальнями гармонируют с красотой окрестностей. Пользующаяся международным признанием за свой функциональный дизайн вилла на острове Бедарра – это место, где расслабленный отдых сочетается с комфортным модернизмом, что непременно отметят истинные ценители стиля!

AUSTRALIA
HERON ISLAND

Surrounded by a kaleidoscope of colourful reefs and shimmering water, Heron Island is outstanding in every respect – a picturesque private island located to the north of Australia's Great Barrier Reef. Popular amongst swimmers, snorkelers and scuba divers alike, this laid-back private island retreat is an abundance of coral gardens and crystal clear waters, perfectly positioned to place all the weird and wonderful creatures of the sea right at your fingertips.

Inmitten eines Kaleidoskops aus farbenfrohen Riffen und glitzerndem Wasser – nördlich von Australiens Great Barrier Reef – liegt Heron Island, eine in jeder Hinsicht außergewöhnliche malerische Privatinsel. Beliebt bei Schwimmern, Schnorchlern und Tauchern ist die Insel ein Wunder mit Korallengärten und kristallklarem Wasser. Die schönen und seltsamen Kreaturen des Ozeans sind hier zum Greifen nah.

Entourée par un kaléidoscope de récifs colorés et d'eaux scintillantes, Heron Island se distingue des autres. Cette île privée spectaculaire et décontractée située au nord de la grande barrière australienne est une destination de choix pour les nageurs et les plongeurs, constellée de jardins de corail et baignée d'eaux cristallines. Idéalement placée sur la route des créatures les plus merveilleuses, vous n'aurez qu'à tendre la main.

Окруженный калейдоскопом красочных рифов и мерцающих волн, остров Херон является выдающимся во всех отношениях – это живописный частный остров, расположенный к северу от Австралийского Большого Барьерного Рифа. Популярный среди пловцов, ныряльщиков и любителей подводного плавания, этот чудесный частный остров отличается изобилием коралловых садов в кристально чистой воде. Благодаря его расположению, можно наблюдать диковинных морских обитателей на расстоянии вытянутой руки.

AUSTRALIA
MAKEPEACE ISLAND

Exclusive and enchanting, Makepeace Island is a heart-shaped island you're sure to fall in love with. Sensitively developed over a number of years, the magnificent Makepeace Island is an exquisite private island hideaway situated just off Queensland's captivating Golden Coast, a heavenly abode with space for up to 22 castaways. For an amazing Australian experience with a distinctly southeast Asian flavour, Richard Branson's antipodean retreat is certain to cast a spell on all those who set foot upon it.

Makepeace Island ist exklusiv und bezaubernd – eine herzförmige Insel – in die man sich sofort verliebt. Über Jahre hinweg liebevoll gestaltet, ist die Privatinsel ein exquisites Refugium vor der faszinierenden Golden Coast Queenslands, das bis zu 22 Gestrandete aufnehmen kann. Ein unvergessliches Australien-Erlebnis gewürzt mit dem besonderen Aroma Südostasiens, Richard Bransons Retreat zieht jeden in seinen Bann.

Chic et enchanteresse, Makepeace Island est une île en forme de cœur dont vous ne manquerez pas de tomber amoureux. Développée au fil des ans avec un soin particulier, cette île magnifique est un sanctuaire privé exquis situé au large de la Golden Coast du Queensland. Capable d'accueillir jusqu'à 22 naufragés volontaires, cette retraite australienne aux accents asiatiques distinctifs charmera tous ceux qui y poseront le pied, à l'image de Richard Branson.

Очаровательный остров Мейкпис, имеющий форму сердца, просто невозможно не полюбить! Этот изысканный частный курорт, тщательно создававшийся в течение многих лет, расположен неподалеку от восхитительного Золотого берега Квинсленда и позволяет разместить до 22 гостей. Удивительный австралийский курорт Ричарда Брэнсона с элементами, напоминающими о юго-восточной Азии, несомненно, очарует всех, кто хоть раз ступил на его берег.

THE NAKA ISLAND

With stunning scenery and covetable views of Thailand's famous Phi Phi Islands, this former fishing village offers much in the way of laid-back luxury. Home to an array of enchanting villas and a sensual spa simply to die for, the tranquil surroundings here are perfect for quiet reflection and rejuvenation. Only five minutes away from the bright lights of Phuket and yet spiritually a world away, The Naka Island is the perfect place to relax and unwind.

Mit einer himmlischen Kulisse und wunderbaren Sicht auf Thailands berühmte Phi Phi Islands, bietet dieses ehemalige Fischerdorf Luxus und Lässigkeit zugleich. Inmitten der ruhigen Umgebung – ideal zur Besinnung und Verjüngung – stehen bezaubernde Villen und ein einfach göttliches Spa. Nur fünf Minuten von den hellen Lichtern Phukets entfernt und doch eine ganz andere Welt – The Naka Island ist ein vollkommener Ort zum Entspannen und Loslassen.

Dans un décor étonnant, à quelques encablures des célèbres îles Phi Phi thaïlandaises, cet ancien village de pêcheurs offre tout le luxe nécessaire à la détente. L'île de Naka abrite plusieurs villas de rêve, ainsi qu'un spa sensuel que vous ne voudrez plus quitter. La tranquillité du lieu, idéale pour la méditation, est une véritable cure de jouvence. À seulement cinq minutes des lumières de Phuket, ce monde spirituel hors du temps est l'endroit parfait pour se détendre et se recentrer.

Этот бывший рыбацкий поселок с потрясающими пейзажами и чудесными видами на знаменитые таиландские острова Пхи-Пхи отличается особой непринужденной роскошью. Здесь находятся очаровательные виллы и спа-центры, которые нужно обязательно увидеть хоть раз в жизни. Спокойная обстановка этого острова идеально подходит для размышлений и восстановления сил. Расположенный всего в пяти минутах от сверкающего Пхукета, но вдали от городской суеты, остров Нака – идеальное место для безмятежного отдыха.

DEDON ISLAND RESORT

Located at the southeastern tip of South Pacific surfers' paradise Siargao, Dedon Island is tucked between ancient mangrove forests, white sands and crystal clear waters – a palm-fringed private island paradise so beautiful that it boggles the mind. Striking a balance between traditional Filipino architecture and the most contemporary of luxury amenities, the island's nine luxury villas are a heady cocktail of rattan chairs, swinging daybeds and other exquisite furniture pieces, sure to delight those with an eye for design.

Dedon Island liegt umgeben von alten Mangrovenwäldern, weißen Stränden und kristallklarem Wasser an der Südostspitze des südpazifischen Surferparadieses Siargao. Die private Insel ist ein palmenbestandenes Stückchen vom Paradies. Neun Luxusvillen verbinden gekonnt philippinische Bautradition mit moderner Luxusausstattung. Die Mischung aus Rattanstühlen, frei schwingenden Ruhebetten und anderem exquisitem Mobiliar erfreut Design-Liebhaber.

Située à la pointe sud-est de Siargo, le paradis des surfeurs du Pacifique Sud, Dedon Island est bordée par d'anciennes mangroves, des plages de sable blanc et des eaux cristallines. La beauté de cette île privée parsemée de palmiers est à couper le souffle. Ce paradis a trouvé l'équilibre parfait entre architecture philippine traditionnelle et confort moderne de luxe. Les neuf somptueuses villas mêlent harmonieusement chaises en rotin, divans à balancelle et autres pièces de mobilier exquis, qui raviront les amateurs de design.

В южной части Тихого океана, на юго-восточном краю Сиаргао, райского уголка для любителей серфинга, спрятался остров Дедон с древними мангровыми зарослями, белыми песками и кристально чистой водой. Этот окаймленный пальмами частный остров отличается невероятной красотой. Здесь имеется девять роскошных вилл, удачно сочетающих в себе традиции филиппинской архитектуры с самыми современными удобствами и роскошью. Истинных ценителей дизайна, несомненно, порадуют плетеные стулья, качающиеся кушетки и другие изысканные предметы обстановки.

PHILIPPINES
ARIARA ISLAND

Hidden in an unexplored area of Far East Asia and yet easily accessible from within the Philippines, there's really no reason not to discover the amazing Ariara Island. Nestled amongst natural beauty and tropical waters, attention has been paid to every last detail on this Filipino favourite, allowing you and up to 17 other guests to enjoy your island getaway concentrating solely on the things you love, whether that be friends, family or simply taking in that soothing South Sea flair.

Gut verborgen in einer unberührten Ecke Fernostasiens und doch von den Philippinen aus leicht zu erreichen – man muss Ariara Island einfach erkunden. Diese beliebte Insel ist umgeben von nichts als Schönheit und tropischen Gewässern, bei der Gestaltung wurde jedes Detail sorgfältig ausgesucht. So können bis zu 18 Gäste sich während ihrer Insel-Auszeit auf die Dinge konzentrieren, die sie lieben: Freunde, Familie oder einfach das süße Flair der Südsee.

Cachée dans une zone inexplorée de l'Extrême-Orient, mais accessible depuis les Philippines, vous vous devez de découvrir l'incroyable île d'Ariara. Nichée au cœur de la nature et entourée d'eaux tropicales, cette retraite a bénéficié de tous les soins. Capable d'accueillir jusqu'à 18 invités, vous pourrez vous y concentrer sur les choses les plus importantes de la vie, que ce soit vos amis, votre famille ou cet instant suspendu dans les mers du sud.

Почему бы вам не открыть для себя удивительный остров Ариара, скрытый в неизведанных областях Дальнего Востока, но легко доступный с Филиппин. На этом острове, скрытом от мира среди природной красоты в тропических водах, могут разместиться до 17 гостей. Здесь продумана каждая деталь для отдыха, и вы можете уделить все внимание самому дорогому, будь это друзья, семья или просто отдых в расслабляющей атмосфере Южного моря.

CAMBODIA
SONG SAA PRIVATE ISLAND

An untamed island far beyond the tourist trail, Song Saa Private Island is Cambodia's first and only luxury island resort: an isolated paradise secluded within a magnificent seascape. Imagine Thailand before it went public and you're halfway there. Blessed with powder-white beaches, verdant rainforests and 27 stunning cottages, great efforts have been taken to preserve the culture and spirit that make this location so unique. Immerse yourself in a new world and put the everyday on hold.

Eine ungezähmte Insel, weit entfernt von den Touristenpfaden. Die private Insel Song Saa ist Kambodschas erstes und einziges Luxus-Insel-Resort: ein ruhiges Paradies im atemberaubenden Ozeanpanorama – ursprünglich wie Thailand vor der Entdeckung. Bei diesem Juwel mit puder-weißen Stränden, grün glitzernden Regenwäldern und 27 bildhübschen Cottages hat man auf die Erhaltung von Kultur und Spirit, die den Zauber der Insel ausmachen, großen Wert gelegt. Man betritt eine andere Welt und lässt die alte zurück.

Cette île indomptée, loin des circuits touristiques, est l'unique installation de luxe au large du Cambodge : un paradis isolé, dans un splendide paysage marin. Imaginez la Thaïlande avant l'ouverture aux touristespour vous faire une idée approximative. Dotée de plages de sable fin, de forêts vierges et de 27 villas époustouflantes, tout a été fait pour préserver la culture et l'esprit de ce lieu unique. Plongez dans le nouveau monde et oubliez votre quotidien.

Расположенный далеко за пределами туристической зоны, дикий частный остров Сонг Саа — это первый и единственный роскошный курорт Камбоджи — уединенный райский уголок, скрытый среди великолепного морского пейзажа. Представьте себе Таиланд до того, как он открылся для туристов, и вы получите некоторое представление о Сонг Саа. На этом сказочном острове с белоснежными пляжами и зеленеющими джунглями имеется 27 потрясающих коттеджей. Здесь были приняты немалые усилия для сохранения культуры и духа острова, которые делают это место уникальным. Погрузитесь с головой в новый мир и забудьте о повседневности.

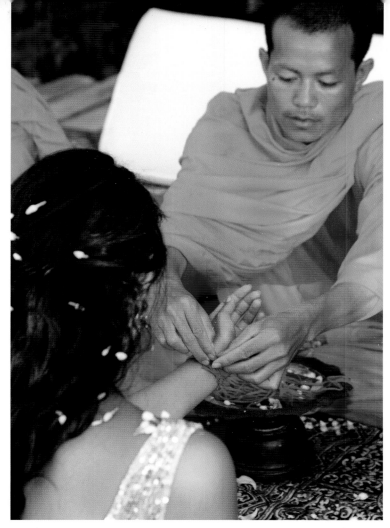

MALAYSIA
PANGKOR LAUT ISLAND

Large enough for adventure, yet small enough to have escaped man's exploitation, Pangkor Laut extends across 300 acres of untamed jungle, with only a fraction of the luscious landscape given over to the island's refined resort. Two million years in the making, and perfectly poised in the Straits of Malacca, Pangkor Laut extolls the heavenly healing culture of this diverse region. Ancient traditions are revived here, sending you on a sensory spa journey which enhances emotional well-being from within.

Die Insel bietet Platz für Abenteuer und ist doch klein genug, um ein Geheimtipp zu bleiben. Pangkor Laut bietet 120 Hektar ursprünglichen Dschungel; für das schicke Island Resort wurde nur ein kleiner Teil der üppigen Vegetation gezähmt. In zwei Millionen Jahren erschaffen und ideal in der Straße von Malakka gelegen, ist Pangkor Laut ein Ort, an dem man die Heilkultur der Region würdigt. Alte Traditionen leben wieder auf und schicken Besucher auf eine Reise der Sinne, bei der das emotionale Wohlbefinden von innen gestärkt wird.

Assez vaste pour donner un sentiment d'aventure, mais suffisamment petite pour avoir échappé à la main de l'homme, Pangkor Laut étire ses 120 hectares de jungle indomptée, dont une infime fraction a été réservée aux installations raffinées de l'hôtel. Âgée de deux millions d'années, posée dans le détroit de Malacca, Pangkor Laut chante les vertus apaisantes de cette région bigarrée. Ici, les traditions renaissent et vous embarquent dans un voyage sensoriel qui ravivera le bien-être émotionnel de l'intérieur.

Достаточно большой для захватывающих приключений, но достаточно маленький, чтобы избежать эксплуатации, Pangkor Laut занимает 300 акров на территории джунглей, где лишь часть роскошного ландшафта передана этому изысканному курорту. Остров, возраст которого составляет 2 млн. лет, гармонично расположен в Малаккском проливе. В спа-салоне можно испытать древние традиции врачевания этого региона для восстановления гармонии и душевных сил.

SRI LANKA
TAPROBANE ISLAND

Occupying a tiny island just off the coast of Sri Lanka, this light and airy four-bedroom octagonal villa was built in the 1920s by the eccentric tea magnate Count de Mauny. Subsequently home to a whole host of literary luminaries, this extraordinary villa is nothing short of a traveller's dream. With its elegant colonial furnishings, countless verandas and stunning swimming pool, Taprobane Island is simultaneously a journey back in time and a journey to another culture.

Auf einer winzigen Insel direkt vor der Küste Sri Lankas hat der exzentrische Teemagnat Count de Mauny in den 20er Jahren diese luftig-leichte, oktogonale Villa mit vier Schlafzimmern erbaut. Später beherbergte die außergewöhnliche Villa diverse literarische Koryphäen und ist heute der wahr gewordene Traum aller Reisenden. Mit der eleganten Kolonialausstattung, zahllosen Veranden und einem atemberaubenden Pool entführt Taprobane Island gleichzeitig in eine andere Zeit und eine andere Kultur.

Sur une petite île au large des côtes du Sri Lanka, cette villa octogonale de quatre chambres aussi légère que spacieuse fut construite dans les années 1920, par le Compte Mauny, magnat excentrique du thé. Elle accueillit par la suite de nombreuses sommités littéraires, véritable rêve de globetrotteur. Dotée d'un élégant mobilier colonial, d'innombrables vérandas et d'une étonnante piscine, Taprobane est aussi bien un voyage dans le passé qu'une découverte culturelle.

Расположенная на крошечном острове недалеко от побережья Шри-Ланки, эта светлая и просторная восьмиугольная вилла с четырьмя спальнями была построена в двадцатых годах эксцентричным чайным магнатом графом де Мони. Впоследствии остров стал традиционным местом отдыха для целого ряда литературных знаменитостей. Эта необыкновенная вилла – настоящая мечта путешественника. Остров Тапробан с элегантной мебелью в колониальном стиле, бесчисленными верандами и потрясающим бассейном одновременно уносит вас в прошлое и приглашает открыть для себя другую культуру.

INDONESIA
KURA KURA RESORT & KRAKAL ISLAND

More than just another private island resort, this dynamic destination gives guests the chance to create their very own castaway experience. Armed with antique petrol lamps, a delicious picnic for two and an all-important sense of adventure, intrepid, would-be Robinson Crusoes will be stranded upon Kura Kura's little sister, Krakal Island, for an unforgettable night under star-speckled skies. Only a short journey from the larger main resort, the combination of comfort and castaway cool truly elevates this private island well above the rest.

Viel mehr als nur ein weiteres Insel-Resort, bietet diese dynamische Privatinsel ihren Gästen die Chance, ihre Robinson-Crusoe-Träume zu leben. Bewaffnet mit antiken Öllampen, einem deliziösen Picknick für zwei und vor allem Abenteuerlust, stranden mutige Besucher auf Kura Kuras kleiner Schwester, Krakal Island, für eine unvergessliche Nacht unterm Sternenhimmel. Nicht weit vom größeren Main Resort entfernt, macht die romantische Mischung aus Schiffbruch-Abenteuer und Komfort diese Insel so besonders.

Plus qu'une simple île privée, cette destination dynamique offre à ses invités la chance de créer leur propre expérience à l'écart du monde. Armé d'antiques lampes à pétrole, d'un savoureux panier pique-nique pour deux et d'un solide sens de l'aventure, l'intrépide Robinson Crusoë qui sommeille en vous ira s'échouer sur la petite sœur de Kura Kura, Krakal, pour une nuit inoubliable sous le ciel étoilé. Non loin des principales installations, le confort et la liberté du lieu le placent bien au-dessus des autres.

Это не просто еще один частный островной курорт – здесь гости могут выбирать стиль своего отдыха. Если у вас есть смелость и страсть к приключениям, и вы хотите ощутить себя Робинзоном Крузо, возьмите антикварные керосиновые лампы, продукты для пикника на двоих, и отправляйтесь на ближайший остров Кракал, чтобы провести незабываемую ночь под звездным небом. Эта короткая поездка с комфортного курорта на уединенный берег придает этому частному острову особый шарм.

INDONESIA
NIKOI ISLAND

Certain to attract up-market adventure lovers, a journey to this picturesque private island is enough transport you back to a land that time forgot. Broadly considered to be the ace up the sleeve of Indonesia's pristine Bintan coast, Nikoi Island is a heady cocktail of poolside perfection and stony sophistication, with ample space for as many as 50 island lovers. With acres of rainforest to explore and a whole host of indulgent experiences, you're free to do as much or as little as you like.

Eine Insel für anspruchsvolle Abenteurer. Eine Reise auf diese pittoreske Privatinsel führt an einen Ort, der von der Zeit vergessen wurde. Nikoi Island – die Trauminsel der ursprünglichen Küste Bintans in Indonesien – bietet bis zu 50 Besuchern vollendete Pool-Idylle im eleganten, felsigen Ambiente. Mit dem Regenwald zum Erkunden und einem reichen Verwöhnprogramm kann man genau so viel oder so wenig unternehmen, wie man möchte.

Les amoureux d'aventure exigeants se laisseront séduire par un voyage vers cette île spectaculaire oubliée par le temps. Atout caché des côtes immaculées de Bintan en Indonésie, l'île de Nikoi est un mélange enivrant de perfection et de sophistication, offrant assez d'espace pour accueillir jusqu'à 50 invités autour de sa piscine, dans un cadre minéral idyllique. Les plaisirs ne manqueront pas et les hectares de forêt vierge n'attendent plus que vous. Vous serez libre de vous activer ou de paresser.

Настоящих любителей приключений, несомненно, привлечет путешествие на живописный частный остров, где время словно остановилось. По праву считающийся жемчужиной побережья Бинтана в Индонезии, остров Никой – это изысканный отдых, отраженный в искрящихся водах бассейна. На этом острове можно разместить до 50 гостей. Разведывая просторы тропического леса или другие интересные места, здесь можно найти занятие по душе или просто предаваться ленивому отдыху.

INDONESIA
PULAU JOYO

Surrounded by soft white sands and vivid blue seas, Pulau Joyo forms a romantic castaway destination set apart from the rest – an incredible island escape sure to soothe the senses and stimulate the mind. Home to a series of innovative driftwood palaces, each somehow dissolving the distinctions between inside and out, the accommodation here captures the very essence of barefoot luxury, providing endless island bliss for up to 30 guests.

Umgeben von weichem, weißem Sand und tiefblauem Wasser ist Pulau Joyo ein romantisches, abgeschiedenes Ziel, das entspannt und die Sinne anregt. In den innovativen Treibholz-Palästen, die die Grenzen zwischen drinnen und draußen verschwimmen lassen, können bis zu 30 Gäste logieren. Ein lockeres Insel-Luxusleben mit einem Versprechen von Glückseligkeit.

Entourée de plages de sable blanc et d'eaux bleues cristallines, Pulau Joyo est une destination reculée romantique à nulle autre pareille. Une île incroyable qui apaise les sens et stimule l'esprit. Elle abrite plusieurs palais de bois flotté innovants, qui brouillent l'espace entre intérieur et extérieur. Ces logements capturent la véritable essence du luxe décontracté, un paradais insulaire capable d'accueillir jusqu'à 30 invités.

Окруженный мягкими белыми песками и синими морями, остров Пулау Джойо – это романтичное и уединенное место для отдыха, которое прекрасно подойдет для романтического путешествия, успокоит ваши чувства и стимулирует разум. Здесь имеется множество удивительных дворцов из коряг, каждый из которых меняет представление о реальности. Это жилье отражает суть истинной роскоши на лоне чудесной островной природы и позволяет разместить до 30 гостей.

AFRICA & INDIAN OCEAN

MALDIVES
NALADHU MALDIVES

Malidivian for "beautiful island", this tiny island more than lives up to its name.
Die maledivische Übersetzung für „schöne Insel" – ein wahrhaft passender Name.
Traduction maldivienne « d'île magnifique » , ce bout de terre n'a pas usurpé son nom.
Этот крохотный островок полностью оправдывает свое название («красивый остров»)
на языке Мальдив.

MALDIVES
ANGSANA IHURU

Angsana Ihuru is your ticket to paradise – a sensory experience like no other.
Angsana Ihuru ist ein Paradies, das alle Sinne berauscht.
Angsana Ihuru est votre billet pour le paradis, une expérience sensorielle sans pareil.
Ангсана Ихуру – это ваш билет в рай, чувственный и единственный в своем роде.

MALDIVES
GILI LANKANFUSHI

MALDIVES
THE BEACH HOUSE AT IRUVELI

Waterslides connect living quarters and luminescent lagoons – start your day with a splash!
Wasserrutschen verbinden die Unterkünfte mit leuchtenden Lagunen – welch ein Erwachen!
Des toboggans relient les quartiers d'habitation aux lagons éteincelants...un réveil en fraicheur !
Водные горки соединяют жилые помещения и сияющие лагуны – начните день всплеском!

Located only metres above glistening turquoise waters – dive in to luxury living.
Nur wenige Meter über dem türkisfarbenen Wasser gelegen – willkommen im Luxusleben.
Située à quelque mètres seulement des eaux turquoise...plongez dans une vie de luxe.
Находясь всего в нескольких метрах над блестящими бирюзовыми водами –
окунитесь в царство роскоши.

SEYCHELLES
BIRD ISLAND LODGE

SEYCHELLES
DENIS ISLAND

An ornithologist's delight, with more than 20 spectacular species to spot.
Ornithologen und Vogelliebhaber finden hier mit über 20 spektakulären Vogelarten ihr Glück.
Paradis des ornithogues, elle offre plus de 20 espèces spectaculaires.
Мечта орнитолога – место, где обитает более 20 живописных видов птиц.

A harmony of natural surroundings, island hospitality and unique Seychellois flair.
Natur, Inselgastfreundschaft und das einzigartige Flair der Seychellen in vollendeter Harmonie.
Située dans un cadre iddylique, cette île des Seychelles offre une hospitalité et une classe unique.
Гармония природного окружения, островное гостеприимство и уникальный

BANYAN TREE MADIVARU

Robinson Crusoe may well have invented castaway chic, but the Banyan Tree Madivaru defines it. Rising with the sun and pushing back the curtains to reveal a pristine stretch of white sand with brilliant blue waters beyond, for those lucky enough to while away the hours within one of the island's six tented pool villas, it could well be a case of love at first sight. With enough to impress even the most seasoned of travellers, the Banyan Tree Madivaru is truly one of the Maldives' premiere destinations.

Robinson Crusoe hat den Gestrandeten-Schick erfunden, doch Banyan Tree Madivaru perfektioniert ihn. Mit der Sonne aufstehen und auf den unberührten weißen Sand vor dem glitzernden blauen Wasser blicken. Alle, die das Glück haben, kostbare Stunden der Muße in einer der sechs zeltartigen Villen mit Pool zu verbringen, verlieben sich wohl auf den ersten Blick. Banyan Tree Madivaru beeindruckt selbst die erfahrensten Reisenden und gehört zu den schicksten Zielen der Malediven.

Robinson Crusoë est peut-être le père du chic insulaire, mais le Banyan Tree Madivaru en est la représentation. Levez-vous avec le soleil, ouvrez les rideaux et découvrez une plage de sable blanc, sur fond de mer bleue et scintillante. Ceux qui auront la chance de paresser dans l'une des six villas avec piscine risquent fort d'en tomber amoureux au premier regard. Banyan Tree Madivaru étourdira les plus avertis des voyageurs et constitue l'une des destinations les plus prestigieuses des Maldives.

Робинзон Крузо, возможно, изобрел шик одиночества, но Banyan Tree Madivaru воплотил его. Встав с первыми лучами сонца и глядя на нетронутый белый песок и сверкающие голубые воды, отодвинув занавески, можно влюбиться в этот остров с первого взгляда. Те, кто проводит время в одной из шести палаточных вилл с бассейном, могут считать, что им действительно повезло. Курорт Banyan Tree Madivaru имеет все для того, чтобы впечатлить даже самого опытного путешественника, и является одним из лучших мест для отдыха на Мальдивах.

COCOA ISLAND BY COMO

A tropical oasis with nothing to distract you from your private island reverie but the sound of the waves gently lapping against the shores below, COMO Cocoa Island boasts stunning accommodation facilities and a spa retreat like no other. Uniquely inspired by traditional Maldivian dhoni boats – the eye-catching wooden vessels used by local fishermen – the 33 incredible overwater villas here stretch out far on to the horizon, forming a lazy curve above the glittering waters of the Indian Ocean.

Eine tropische Oase. Begleitet vom sanften Plätschern der Wellen kann man sich ganz seinen Inselträumen hingeben. COMO Cocoa Island bietet atemberaubende Unterkünfte und ein Spa Retreat, das es so nur einmal gibt. Inspiriert von den traditionellen Dhonis der Malediven – den hübschen Fischerbooten der Einheimischen – erstrecken sich 33 ins Wasser gebaute Villen in einem sanften Bogen über dem glitzernden Indischen Ozean weit bis zum Rand des Horizonts.

Cocoa Island de COMO est une oasis tropicale, une rêverie insulaire protégée, bercée par le son des vagues qui viennent caresser ses côtes. Elle vous offre un hébergement remarquable, ainsi qu'un spa sans pareil. Inspirées par les dhonis traditionnels des Maldives, les étonnants navires encore utilisées par les pêcheurs locaux, les 33 villas sur pilotis s'ouvrent sur l'horizon, formant une courbe langoureuse sur les eaux scintillantes de l'Océan Indien.

Курорт Cocoa Island by COMO — это тропический оазис, где ничто не отвлекает вас от мечтательных грез на личном острове, кроме шороха волн, мягко ласкающих берег. COMO Cocoa Island отличается великолепными условиями проживания и превосходными спа-процедурами. 33 уникальные виллы над водой своим видом напоминают традиционные мальдивские лодки «дхони», используемые местными рыбаками. Ряд вилл тянется далеко за горизонт, формируя плавный изгиб над сверкающими водами Индийского океана.

MALDIVES
COCO PRIVÉ KUDA HITHI ISLAND

Perched within some of the world's most pristine waters, atop a vast underwater mountain range, the North Malé Atoll is truly a thing of beauty. Emerging from the depths of the Indian Ocean like a dream, Coco Privé Kuda Hithi Island is the quintessential Maldives island escape – an entire private island dedicated to you. Discover a world where luxury and serenity walk hand in hand: your home away from home. Give in to a sensual sanctuary for up to twelve castaways.

Das Nord-Malé-Atoll ruht in einem der unberührtesten Wasser der Welt an der Spitze eines gewaltigen Unterwassergebirges und ist ein wahres Wunder an Schönheit. Aus den Tiefen des Indischen Ozeans aufgetaucht wie eine Fata Morgana, ist Coco Privé Kuda Hithi Island der Inbegriff einer Malediven-Auszeit. Eine Privatinsel zum allein Genießen. Hier offenbart sich eine Welt, in der Luxus und Gelassenheit Hand in Hand gehen: ein sinnlicher Zufluchtsort für zwölf Gestrandete.

Perchée sur des eaux cristallines, au sommet d'une chaîne de montagnes sous-marine, l'atoll de North Malé est une vision paradisiaque. Émergeant des profondeurs de l'Océan Indien tel un rêve, le Coco Privé Kuda Hithi Island est la quintessence de l'évasion...une île privée à votre entière disposition. Découvrez un monde où luxe et sérénité vont de pair. Laissez-vous emporter par la sensualité de ce sanctuaire, réservé à douze invités.

Расположенный в самых чистых водах в мире, на вершине огромного подводного горного хребта, атолл Северный Мале — это само воплощение красоты. Возникая, как сон, из глубины Индийского океана, остров Коко-Приве-Куда-Хитхи является квинтэссенцией отдыха на Мальдивских островах — весь частный остров находится в вашем распоряжении! Откройте для себя мир роскоши и безмятежности, свой дом вдали от дома. Предайтесь чувственному отдыху в уединенном райском уголке для 12 гостей.

MALDIVES
ISLAND HIDEAWAY AT DHONAKULHI

Located only a few metres above glistening turquoise waters, the Island Hideaway at Dhonakulhi promises unspoilt beauty from every corner. Part of the exclusive Haa Alif atoll, this spectacular island is a million miles from the everyday, promising sensual seclusion for all those who set foot upon her. With a luxury boutique resort and a team of discrete and attentive butlers always on hand to cater to your every need, life couldn't be easier in this alluring idyll.

Island Hideaway at Dhonakulhi liegt nur wenige Meter über dem glitzernden türkisfarbenen Wasser und verheißt Schönheit, wohin das Auge blickt. Teil des exklusiven Haa-Alif-Atolls, ist diese spektakuläre Insel Millionen Kilometer vom Alltag entfernt und verspricht sinnliche Zurückgezogenheit für alle, die einen Fuß auf ihre Küsten setzen. Mit einem luxuriösen Boutique Resort und diskreten Bediensteten, die Wünsche von den Augen ablesen, könnte das Leben in diesem verführerischen Paradies nicht schöner sein.

À quelques mètres seulement au-dessus des eaux turquoise scintillantes, l'Island Hideaway de Dhonakulhi vous offre une beauté préservée. Dans l'atoll privé de Haa Alif, cette île spectaculaire est à un million de kilomètres de votre quotidien, un sanctuaire de sensualité qui vous ravira. Avec une boutique de luxe et une équipe de majordomes discrets prêts à vous servir, la vie ne pourrait être plus douce qu'en ce lieu idyllique.

Расположенный всего в нескольких метрах над сверкающими бирюзовыми водами, спа-курорт на острове Дхонакули отличается нетронутой красотой. Будучи частью эксклюзивного рифа Хаа Алиф, этот великолепный остров гарантирует своим гостям сладостное уединение. Этот роскошный курорт-бутик предлагает услуги внимательных личных дворецких, которые готовы удовлетворить любые ваши желания. Каждый день на этом идиллическом острове – настоящий праздник!

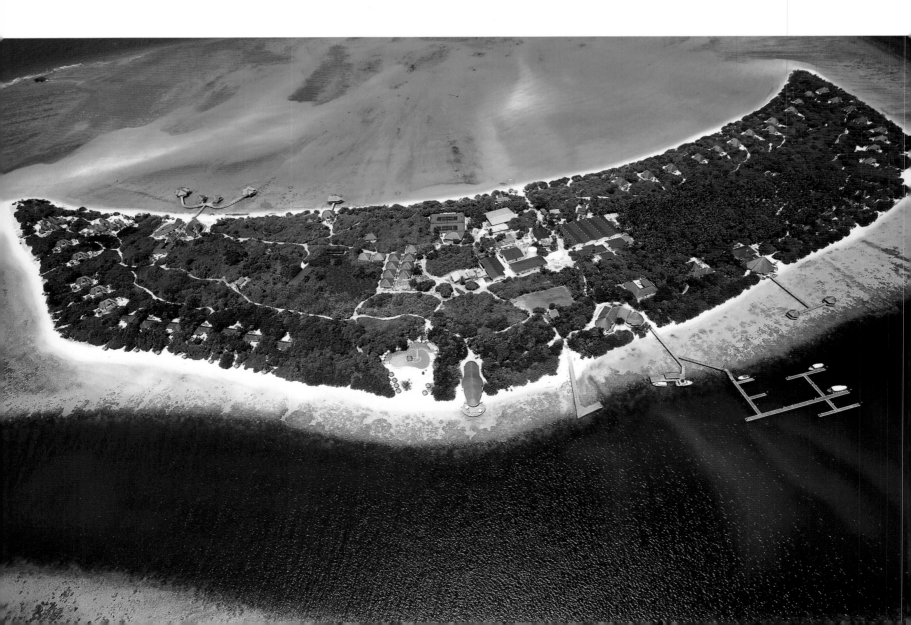

MIRIHI ISLAND RESORT

Popular with loved-up couples and diving fanatics alike, the magical Mirihi Island Resort is an enchanting emerald gem which simply exudes exoticism. Home to scores of swaying palm trees and a luminous lagoon, Mirihi is a picture-book private island in every respect. Dive head first in to the warm waters of the South Ari Atoll and revel in the delights of the house reef, where a kaleidoscope of colours, corals and vibrant marine life await your discovery.

Ein Favorit der frisch Verliebten und Tauchfanatiker ist das magische Mirihi Island Resort. Ein bezaubernder Smaragd, der mit seiner Exotik verführt. Mit unzähligen Palmen und einer leuchtenden Lagune ist Mirihi in jeder Hinsicht eine Privatinsel wie aus dem Bilderbuch. Ein Kopfsprung ins warme Wasser des Süd-Ari-Atolls offenbart die Wunderwelt des Riffs. Ein Kaleidoskop aus Farben, Korallen und reichem Unterwasserleben möchte entdeckt werden.

La magie de Mirihi Island Resort enchantera aussi bien les couples enivrés d'amour que les amateurs de plongée, une émeraude aux parfums exotiques. Abritant d'innombrables palmiers langoureux, ainsi qu'un lagon lumineux, Mirihi est une île privée féerique. Plongez dans ses eaux chaudes au sud de l'atoll d'Ari et découvrez les merveilles du récif, véritable kaléidoscope de couleurs, de coraux et de poissons bigarrés.

Популярный среди романтических пар и любителей дайвинга, волшебный курорт острова Мирихи – это настоящее экзотическое сокровище, затерянное в изумрудных водах. Кажется, что этот чудесный остров с его качающимися пальмами и сверкающей лагуной сошел с картинки. Окунитесь с головой в теплые воды атолла Южный Ари и наслаждайтесь прелестями прибрежного рифа, где вас ждет настоящий калейдоскоп красок, кораллов и ярких морских обитателей.

MALDIVES
ONE&ONLY REETHI RAH

Home to some of the largest resort villas the world over, the One&Only Reethi Rah is the unparalleled choice of discerning island travellers. Set on one of the largest islands in the North Malé Atoll and adorned with endless white sand and turquoise bays, this impressive island escape is one of the most sought-after destinations across the whole of the Maldives. A favourite haunt amongst the gliteratti, you never know who you might bump into in the Reethi restaurant.

Eine der größten Resort-Villen der Welt erwartet Besucher auf One&Only Reethi Rah, einem einzigartigen Ziel für anspruchsvolle Insel-Reisende. Auf einer der größten Inseln des Nord-Malé-Atolls, geschmückt mit endlosen weißen Sandstränden und türkisfarbenen Buchten, thront dieses beeindruckende Resort und ist eines der beliebtesten Ziele der Malediven. An diesem Lieblingsort der Reichen und Schönen weiß man nie, wer einem im Reethi-Restaurant begegnen mag.

One&Only Reethi Rah abrite quelques-unes des villas les plus vastes au monde, une destination de choix pour voyageurs exigeants. Sur l'une des plus grandes îles de l'atoll de Malé, entourée de longues plages de sable blanc et de baies turquoise, cette île est l'une des plus prisées dans toutes les Maldives. Sanctuaire de prédilection des stars, qui sait qui vous pourriez rencontrer au restaurant du Reethi...

Курорт One&Only Reethi Rah с его крупнейшими в мире курортными виллами – это идеальный выбор даже для самых опытных и взыскательных путешественников. Расположенный на одном из самых больших островов рифа Северный Мале, остров славится своим бесконечным белым песком и бирюзовыми заливами. Это чудесное место является одним из самых престижных курортов на всей территории Мальдивских островов. Это также излюбленное место для отдыха среди знаменитостей, и здесь вы никогда не знаете, с кем из них вы столкнетесь в ресторане.

SONEVA FUSHI

Whilst words and images stoke the imagination, the only way to truly get to know this exceptional island is to experience it. So far away from it all, and yet so close to home, Soneva Fushi is the original tropical island escape. With perfect powder-soft beaches, crystal-clear waters, and a dense jungle interwoven with intricate wooden pathways, there are few more beautiful locations on earth. Isn't it about time you discovered the magic for yourself?

Worte können die Magie dieser besonderen Insel nicht beschreiben, man muss sie selbst erleben. Weit entfernt von allem und doch so nah ist Soneva Fushi eine Tropeninsel wie aus dem Bilderbuch. Vollkommene puderweiche Strände, kristallklares Wasser und ein dichter, von hölzernen Pfaden durchzogener Dschungel machen diesen Ort zu einem der schönsten der Erde. Die Insel wartet darauf, Sie zu verzaubern...

Si les mots et les images alimentent l'imagination, le seul véritable moyen de découvrir cette île exceptionnelle n'est encore que de vous y rendre. Éloignée de tout, et pourtant si proche, Soneva Fushi est une véritable échappée insulaire tropicale. Avec ses plages de sable blanc immaculé, ses eaux cristallines et une jungle dense parcourue de sentiers balisés, il existe peu de destinations aussi féeriques au monde. Il est temps pour vous de venir découvrir la magie par vous-même...

Хотя слова и образы разжигают воображение, единственный способ по-настоящему узнать этот исключительный остров — это побывать на нем. Вдали от всего, и все же так близко к дому, курорт Soneva Fushi — это оригинальное место для отдыха на тропическом острове. Изумительные пляжи с шелковистым песком, кристально чистые воды, густые джунгли с замысловатыми деревянными мостками... в мире найдется немного столь красивых мест. Разве не время открыть для себя этот волшебный мир?

SEYCHELLES
FRÉGATE ISLAND PRIVATE

Whoever said life is about the journey, not the destination, clearly never visited Frégate Island Private. A sanctuary of seclusion where dreams come true and memories are made; Frégate is arguably the original barefoot luxury island. Home to some of the world's most celebrated beaches, this award-winning island cannot fail to delight. Secluded by a lush palm jungle, each of the 16 impressive residence villas promises limitless luxury and exclusivity that draws back the A-listers year after year.

Wer gesagt hat, im Leben gehe es um den Weg, nicht um das Ziel, hat niemals Frégate Island besucht. Ein Ort vollkommener Abgeschiedenheit, an dem Träume wahr und Erinnerungen fürs Leben geboren werden. Frégate ist der Inbegriff des entspannten Luxuslebens. Mit einigen der beliebtesten Strände der Welt, begeistert die preisgekrönte Insel immer. Geschützt von einem üppigen Palmendschungel, verspricht jede der 16 beeindruckenden Villen Luxus ohne Grenzen und eine Exklusivität, die Kenner immer wiederkehren lässt.

Quiconque a un jour déclaré que la vie était un voyage, non une destination, n'a clairement jamais posé le pied sur Frégate Island Private. Ce sanctuaire de tranquillité où le rêve devient réalité et où les souvenirs se créent est sans doute l'incarnation du luxe décontracté. Frégate abrite quelques-unes des plages les plus célèbres au monde. Reconnue pour sa grande beauté, elle ne manquera pas de vous ravir. Nichées dans une jungle luxuriante, les 16 impressionnantes villas vous garantissent un luxe et un calme sans pareil, comme l'attestent les habitués les plus prestigieux du lieu.

Тот, кто сказал, что жизнь – это путешествие, а не пункт назначения, наверняка никогда не бывал на частном острове Фрегат. Это уединенный райский уголок, где сбываются мечты и создаются воспоминания, который некоторые считают самым первым островом, где роскошные условия сочетаются с проживанием на лоне природы. Этот удостоенный наград остров, где находятся некоторые самые известные в мире пляжи, не разочарует своих гостей! 16 роскошных вилл, укрытых в пышных пальмовых джунглях, каждый год привлекают сюда самых знаменитых и богатых путешественников.

SEYCHELLES
NORTH ISLAND

You could spend a lifetime searching for a destination as divine as this. The only place to go when perfection won't suffice, North Island is truly a temple of indulgence, an opulent escape for up to 22 guests, whose highlight is without a doubt the fabled Villa eleven – a 750 square metres palace which cascades gracefully along granite boulders before coming to rest on a pristine, private beach below. A residence fit for a king, the Duke and Duchess of Cambridge spent their honeymoon here, giving the island a royal seal of approval in the process.

North Island ist einzigartig und schlicht vollkommen. Ein wahrer Tempel des Genusses, ein opulentes Refugium für 22 Gäste. Höhepunkt ist die sagenhafte Villa elf – ein 750 Quadratmeter großer Palast – der sich majestätisch über Granitfelsen bis hin zum unberührten Privatstrand erstreckt. Herzog und Herzogin von Cambridge haben ihre Flitterwochen hier verbracht und der Insel das königliche Gütesiegel verliehen.

Vous pourriez passez une vie entière à chercher un lieu aussi divin que celui-ci. Lorsque la perfection ne suffit plus, North Island exaucera les vœux des plus exigeants, un véritable temple du plaisir, une escapade opulente pour 22 invités. La fabuleuse villa onze, un palais de 750 mètres carrés qui glisse gracieusement le long d'énormes blocs de granit pour venir reposer sur une plage privée immaculée en atteste. Cette résidence royale eut l'honneur de recevoir le Duc et la Duchesse de Cambridge pour leur lune de miel, qui lui offrirent ainsi ses lettres de noblesse.

Такое божественное место встречается лишь раз в жизни. Когда никакое совершенство не удовлетворяет, Северный остров остается вершиной роскоши и удовольствий. На этом великолепном острове можно разместить до 22 гостей. Неизгладимое впечатление оставляет легендарный дворец «Villa 11» площадью 750 кв.м с изящными каскадами гранитных валунов, спускающимися к девственному частному пляжу. В этой поистине королевской резиденции провели свой медовый месяц герцог и герцогиня Кембриджские, давшие острову королевский знак одобрения.

SEYCHELLES
COUSINE ISLAND

In the azure waters of the Indian Ocean there is an island like no other...an island where wildlife thrives and man is a mere observer of Mother Nature's miracles. A luxury getaway unlike any other, Cousine recently emerged from an extraordinary renovation whilst successfully keeping its spirit very much intact. Recognised internationally as one of the world's most ecologically important private islands, Cousine Island is an environmental experience sure to leave guests with a sense of belonging to nature.

Im azurblauen Wasser des Indischen Ozeans schwimmt eine Insel wie keine andere. Eine Insel, auf der die Tierwelt gedeiht und der Mensch die Wunder der Natur bestaunt. Ein Luxusrefugium ohnegleichen, das gerade einer außerordentlichen Umgestaltung unterzogen wurde, bei der das magische Flair des Ortes erfolgreich bewahrt wurde. International anerkannt als eine der wichtigsten Privatinseln aus ökologischer Sicht, ist Cousine Island ein Erlebnis, das seine Gäste wieder mit der Natur vereint.

Dans les eaux azur de l'Océan Indien navigue une île à nulle autre pareille...une île où l'homme peut observer la vie sauvage en ébullition. Cousine est un luxueux sanctuaire, résultat d'une somptueuse rénovation qui a su conserver l'esprit du lieu. Reconnue à travers le monde comme l'une des îles privées les plus écologiquement importantes, Cousine est une expérience environnementale qui resserrera les liens des invités avec Mère nature.

В лазурных водах Индийского океана находится удивительный остров, не похожий ни на какой другой... Это настоящее царство дикой природы, где человек — всего лишь наблюдатель ее чудес. Этот удивительный курорт был недавно переоборудован, но при этом сохранил свое неповторимое очарование. Остров Кузин по праву считается одним из самых экологически значимых частных островов во всем мире. Проживание на острове подарит гостям ощущение близости к природе.

SEYCHELLES
DESROCHES ISLAND RESORT

Located within the breath-taking Amirante Islands – a region so beautiful it was once confused with the Garden of Eden itself – Desroches Island is so picturesque that it plays with the imagination. Passionately protected by the Seychelles government, only sustainable development is permitted here, allowing travellers to experience the life of a castaway without compromising their green ideals. With a sensual spa devoted to the rejuvenation of body and soul, this island will take you to seventh heaven.

Inmitten der atemberaubenden Amirante Islands – einer Region, die so schön ist, dass sie einst mit dem Garten Eden verwechselt wurde – liegt Desroches Island. Die Insel scheint fast unwirklich in ihrer Schönheit. Von der Regierung der Seychellen sorgfältig beschützt, ist hier nur nachhaltige Entwicklung erlaubt. So können Reisende die Insel in völliger Harmonie mit ihren Umweltidealen erleben. Auch dank dem sinnlichen Spa, das sich der Verjüngung von Körper und Seele widmet, schwebt man hier im siebten Himmel.

Au cœur des Amirantes, une région si merveilleuse que les premiers explorateurs la prirent pour le jardin d'Eden, Desroches est si époustouflante qu'elle joue avec les sens. Protégée avec passion par le gouvernement des Seychelles, seul un développement durable y est autorisé. Les voyageurs pourront ainsi profiter de la solitude, sans compromettre leurs idéaux écologiques. Avec son spa voué au rajeunissement du corps et de l'esprit, cette île vous emportera au septième ciel.

Амирантские острова настолько красивы, что однажды их приняли за сад Эдема, а сам остров Дерош так живописен, что пробуждает воображение. Он ревностно охраняется сейшельским правительством, и здесь разрешены только экологичные проекты, в результате чего путешественники могут наслаждаться отдыхом без ущерба для местной сказочной природы. А благодаря роскошным спа-салонам вы сможете восстановить физические и душевные силы и почувствовать себя на седьмом небе.

^MAURITIUS
ÎLE DES DEUX COCOS

From exhilarating adventures to inspirational landscapes and cultural experiences, Île des Deux Cocos has redefined the tropical resort experience to portray a celebration of island life at its lightest and brightest. Ideal for couples or small families, this pristine private island is perfectly positioned off the coast of Mauritius, rising from the sun-speckled sapphire waters of the Indian Ocean like a beacon, calling you to paradise. Once seen, never forgotten.

Ob aufregende Abenteuer, inspirierende Landschaften und kulturelle Erlebnisse, die Île des Deux Cocos hat die Tropen-Resort-Erfahrung ganz neu definiert. Hier feiert man das Inselleben von seiner schönsten und leuchtendsten Seite. Diese ursprüngliche, perfekt vor der Küste Mauritius' gelegene Insel ist ideal für Paare oder kleine Familien. Schön wie ein Trugbild ragt sie aus dem sonnengefleckten, smaragdgrünen Wasser empor – wer sie sieht, muss sich verlieben.

Terre d'aventures exaltantes, de paysages époustouflants et d'expériences culturelles, l'Île des Deux Cocos redéfinit le concept d'hébergement tropical et célèbre la vie insulaire de façon aussi lumineuse que paisible. Parfaite pour les couples ou les petites familles, cette île privée immaculée est idéalement placée au large des côtes de l'île Maurice sur les eaux saphir scintillantes de l'Océan Indien. Ce phare naturel vous indique l'entrée du paradis. La voir, c'est l'adopter.

От веселых приключений до впечатляющих пейзажей, курорт Île des Deux Cocos оставляет незабываемое впечатление от проживания на острове и идеально подходит для влюбленных пар или небольших семей. Этот девственный частный остров расположен недалеко от берегов острова Маврикий. Он вырастает, как маяк, из искрящихся изумрудных вод Индийского Океана и зовет в свои объятия. Увидев хоть раз, его невозможно забыть.

CONSTANCE TSARABANJINA MADAGASCAR

Perfect for those who like to stray from the beaten path, the Constance Tsarabanjina Madagascar is the epitome of barefoot luxury. Ringed by white sandy beaches and ensconced within a calm canvas of sapphire skies and celadon waters, the 25 bungalows on this intoxicating island are the perfect places to relax, recover and unwind. Sensual spa treatments and mesmerising massages make this magical Madagascan destination all the more memorable – truly a tonic for the soul.

Ideal für alle, die gern die ausgetretenen Pfade verlassen. Constance Tsarabanjina Madagascar ist der Inbegriff des lässigen Luxuslebens. Umrahmt von weißen Sandstränden und geborgen zwischen blauem Himmel und grün-schillerndem Ozean sind die 25 Bungalows perfekt, um zu entspannen und loszulassen. Die herrlichen Spa-Behandlungen und Massagen sind – wie die ganze Insel – eine wahre Erfrischung für die Seele.

Conçue pour ceux qui préfèrent s'écarter des sentiers battus, Constance Tsarabanjina Madagascar est l'apogée du luxe décontracté. Entourés de plages de sable blanc, nichés dans un écrin tranquille de ciel azur et d'eaux céladon, les 25 bungalows de cette île enivrante invitent à la détente, au calme et à l'apaisement. Les traitements sensuels du spa et les massages hypnotiques qui vous seront proposés feront de cette destination magique un lieu inoubliable...un vrai tonifiant spirituel.

Идеальный выбор для тех, кто любит отклоняться от проторенных путей, мадагаскарский курорт Constance Tsarabanjina – это воплощение естественной роскоши на лоне природы. Окруженные белыми песчаными пляжами, на фоне безмятежных голубых небес и лазурных волн, уютно расположены 25 бунгало. Этот опьяняющий остров – идеальное место для отдыха, восстановления сил и расслабления. Чувственные спа-процедуры и поистине волшебные массажи делают это удивительное место на Мадагаскаре неповторимым. Это настоящий бальзам для души!

&BEYOND
MNEMBA ISLAND LODGE

Located just off the tip of northern Zanzibar, this secluded, sun-soaked island hideaway is certain to appeal to any young romantics. Whether as a relaxing end to an exhilarating safari or as an island escape in its own right, the beautiful &Beyond Mnemba Island Lodge is a rare haven, capable of affording travellers with the time and space to forget the rest of the world. If you can tear yourself away from the island's ten luxury bandas, why not take a trip out to one of the island's sensational sandbanks and enjoy a picturesque picnic for two?

Vor der Spitze Nordsansibars verbirgt sich diese sonnenverwöhnte Perle, die besonders frisch Verliebte in ihren Bann zieht. Entspannung, Safari-Abenteuer oder einfach eine Inselauszeit, die bildschöne &Beyond Mnemba Island Lodge ist ein seltener Hafen, in dem Reisende alles finden, um den Rest der Welt für eine Weile zu vergessen. Schafft man es, sich von den zehn luxuriösen Bandas zu entfernen, bieten sich ein Ausflug zu einer der sensationellen Sandbänke oder ein Picknick zu zweit vor malerischer Kulisse an.

Située à la pointe nord de Zanzibar, cette île reculée baignée de soleil ravira les jeunes romantiques. Lieu de détente ou de départ vers un safari exaltant, la magnifique &Beyond Mnemba Island Lodge est un havre de tranquillité à l'écart du monde. Elle offira aux voyageurs le temps et l'espace pour oublier leur quotidien. Si vous parvenez à quitter les dix luxueuses bandas de l'île, pourquoi ne pas rejoindre l'une des sensationnelles plages, pour profiter d'un pique-nique idyllique à deux ?

Расположенное возле северной границы Занзибара, это уединенное, пропитанное солнцем островное убежище наверняка понравится молодым романтикам. Будь это расслабляющее завершение увлекательного сафари или островной отдых сам по себе, чудесный домик на острове Мнемба от компании &Beyond предоставит путешественникам новое измерение времени и пространства, чтобы заставить их забыть внешний мир. А если вы все же сможете вырваться из объятий роскоши десяти островных домиков, то почему бы не отправиться на одну из знаменитых отмелей острова и не устроить там живописный пикник на двоих?

MOZAMBIQUE
VAMIZI ISLAND

A slender coral island off Mozambique's remote northern coast, Vamizi Island is an insider's tip for travellers searching for pure relaxation and incredible diving conditions. Home to 13 spectacular villas located along soft, secluded sands, the astounding accommodation here creates an atmosphere that merges perfectly with its surrounding environment. Warm welcomes, chic styling and Mozambican flair ensure an African vacation with a twist in the tail.

Eine hübsche Koralleninsel vor Mosambiks Nordküste. Vamizi Island ist ein Geheimtipp für Reisende, die absolute Entspannung und fabelhafte Tauchbedingungen suchen. Auf die Gäste warten 13 wunderschöne Villen an friedvollen, weißen Sandstränden, in perfekter Harmonie mit der sie umgebenden Natur. Das herzliche Willkommen, schicke Design und der Zauber Mosambiks sorgen für einen Afrika-Urlaub der besonderen Art.

Cette élégante île corallienne au large de la côte nord du Mozambique est un secret bien gardé que les voyageurs à la recherche de détente et de conditions de plongée de prestige sauront apprécier. Vamizi abrite 13 villas spectaculaires, situées le long de plages reculées. L'hébergement haut de gamme crée une atmosphère en harmonie avec l'environnement. La chaleur, le chic et le style du Mozambique vous garantiront des vacances africaines étonnantes.

Вытянутый коралловый остров Вамизи возле удаленного северного побережья Мозамбика – это идеальное место для тех, кто ищет условия для дайвинга и полноценного отдыха. 13 захватывающих вилл, расположенных вдоль уединенного побережья с шелковистым песком, создают атмосферу полного слияния с окружающей природой. Теплый прием, изысканный дизайн и особый мозамбикский стиль сделают ваш африканский отпуск незабываемым.

EUROPE

NORWAY
LØKSØYA

Excellent angling opportunities and awe-inspiring views of the Aurora Borealis.
Exzellente Angelbedingungen und atemberaubende Sicht auf das Polarlicht des Nordens.
Pour les amateurs de pêche à la ligne, sous d'impressionnantes aurores boréales.
Отличные возможности для рыбалки и впечатляющие виды Северного Сияния.

IRELAND
FOTA ISLAND RESORT

Fota Island Resort is the whole package—ideal for a wicked weekend break.
Fota Island Resort – ein Wochenendziel mit vielen Möglichkeiten.
Fota Island Resort a tout pour elle, idéale pour un petit week-end crapuleux.
На курорте Fota Island Resort имеется все необходимое, чтобы назвать его идеальным местом для отдыха в выходные.

SWEDEN
DÄMMANS FYR

Discover Dämmans Fyr—a beautiful lighthouse island surrounded by swirling waters.
Dämmans Fyr ist ein schönes Leuchtturm-Eiland inmitten wirbelnder Wasser.
Découvrez Dämmans Fyr et son magnifique phare entouré d'eaux tourbillonnantes.
Откройте для себя этот красивый остров с маяком, окруженный водоворотами.

FRANCE
COSTAÉRÈS

Eccentric and enchanting in equal measure—a fairy-tale location like no other.
Exzentrisch und bezaubernd zugleich – ein märchenhafter Ort.
Aussi excentrique que séduisante, une destination féerique sans pareil.
Эксцентричное и чудесное место, похожее на волшебную сказку.

GREAT BRITAIN
TRESCO ISLAND

Palm trees, beaches and cobalt blue waters—it's England, but not as you know it!
Palmen, Strände und tiefblaues Wasser – das ist England, aber anders, als man es kennt!
Des palmiers, des plages et des eaux bleu-cobalt...l'Angleterre comme vous ne la connaissiez pas !
Пальмы, пляжи и кобальтовая синь воды – это Англия, но не такая, какой вы ее знаете!

IRELAND
WATERFORD CASTLE HOTEL & GOLF RESORT

Perfectly poised within the King's Channel and only moments away from Waterford City, this luxury 310-acre private island certainly has the wow-factor. Romantic river panoramas complement the well-tended gardens and greens, whereas an ancient castle imposes an incredible sense of history upon all those who cross its threshold. The grand designs and regal fittings of the island's luxury lodgings are simply breathtaking, whereas the Presidential Suite will leave you feeling like the star of a classic costume drama.

Mitten im King's Channel gelegen und nur Augenblicke von Waterford City entfernt, hat diese 125 Hektar große Luxus-Privatinsel ihre ganz eigenen Wunder. Romantische Flusspanoramen vervollständigen die gepflegten Gärten und ein altes Schloss entführt alle, die über seine Schwelle treten, in vergangene Zeiten. Die prächtigen Designs und königliche Ausstattung der luxuriösen Unterkünfte sind überwältigend. In der Presidential Suite fühlt man sich als Held eines klassischen Theaterstücks.

Idéalement placée dans le King's Channel, à quelques minutes seulement de Waterford City, cette île privée de luxe de plus de 125 hectares vous stupéfiera. Des rivières romantiques soulignent les jardins soignés, tandis que l'ancien château impose tout le poids de son histoire sur ceux qui passeront le pas de sa grande porte. L'architecture et le faste des logements de luxe sont à couper le souffle. Découvrez également la Suite Présidentielle et imaginez-vous au beau milieu d'une pièce classique en costume.

Расположенный в Королевском канале, всего в нескольких минутах от города Уотерфорд, этот чудесный частный остров площадью 310 акров не может не вызвать восхищения. Романтичные речные панорамы прекрасно дополняют ухоженные сады и зелень, а старинный замок дает невероятное ощущение истории всем, кто переступает его порог. Впечатляющая архитектура и королевская обстановка роскошных помещений просто завораживают, а в президентском номере вы почувствуете себя актером исторического фильма.

SCOTLAND
ISLE OF ERISKA

Nestled on the eastern side of one of the world's most famous rift valleys and born of cataclysmic upheavals which took place more than 600 million years ago, the Isle of Eriska offers luxurious five-star accommodation with a view to match. With an unbelievably attentive service, award-winning hearty cuisine and 300 acres of stunning Scottish Highland scenery to enjoy, the Isle of Eriska is a holy trinity of peace, comfort and tranquillity, enticing island explorers back year after year – whatever the weather.

Vor 600 Millionen Jahren aus kataklysmischen Umwälzungen geboren, schmiegt sich die Isle of Eriska an die Ostseite des berühmtesten Grabenbruchs der Welt und bietet Besuchern luxuriöse 5-Sterne-Unterkünfte mit einmaliger Aussicht. Hier genießen Sie höchst aufmerksamen Service, eine preisgekrönte Küche und 121 Hektar herrliche schottische Landschaft. Mit ihrer Mischung aus Frieden, Ruhe und Komfort lockt die Insel ihre Besucher jedes Jahr zurück, egal, bei welchem Wetter.

Nichée sur le flanc du plus célèbre rift et née d'une série de cataclysmes vieux de plus de 600 millions d'années, l'île d'Eriska offre des logements cinq étoiles et une vue sans pareil. Un service incroyablement attentif, une cuisine reconnue pour sa qualité et 121 hectares de paysages de Highlands écossais viennent souligner la sainte trinité d'Eriska...paix, confort et tranquillité. Quel que soit le temps, elle attire les explorateurs, année après année.

На восточной стороне одной из самых знаменитых рифтовых долин находится остров Эриска, возникший более 600 миллионов лет назад в результате катастрофических потрясений. Здесь предлагаются пятизвездочные номера с роскошными видами, исключительно внимательное обслуживание и превосходная кухня, удостоенная наград. Радуют глаз великолепные пейзажи Шотландского высокогорья, расположенного на 300 акрах земли. Остров Эриска – это символ спокойствия, комфорта и расслабления, привлекающий исследователей островов, которые возвращаются сюда год за годом – в любую погоду.

SCOTLAND
SANDA ISLAND

This rural retreat is home to a small farm, a remote public house and even a picturesque lighthouse – the perfect stage for watching Scotland's ever-changing coastal scenery. Owned by a Swedish family and an international property developer, Sanda has recently undergone an impressive transformation that has brought the island into the 21st century whilst still retaining its unique rustic charm. A heady mix of pure nature, luxurious comfort and fine dining, the food on Sanda Island is second to none.

Das ländliche Refugium mit einer kleinen Farm, einer abgeschiedenen Gastwirtschaft und einem malerischen Leuchtturm ist die perfekte Kulisse, um den steten Wandel von Schottlands Küstenlandschaft zu bestaunen. Das Eigentum einer schwedischen Familie und eines internationalen Bauherrn wurde jüngst liebevoll mit dem Komfort des 21. Jahrhunderts ausgestattet, wobei der einzigartige rustikale Charme bewahrt wurde. Eine gelungene Mischung aus Natur, luxuriösem Komfort und feiner Küche.

Cette retraite rurale abrite une petite ferme, une auberge isolée et un phare pittoresque...l'endroit rêvé pour admirer le paysage côtier changeant d'Écosse. Propriété d'une famille suédoise et d'un promoteur international, Sanda a récemment subi une impressionnante transformation, qui a fait bondir l'île dans le XXIe siècle, tout en préservant son charme rustique. Mélange enivrant de nature, de confort luxueux et de cuisine fine, Sanda Island n'a pas d'égale.

На этом сельском курорте имеется небольшая ферма, удаленный трактир и даже живописный маяк, с которого можно наблюдать за постоянно меняющимися прибрежными пейзажами Шотландии. Остров принадлежит шведской семье и международному застройщику. Недавние преобразования на острове Санда перенесли его в 21 век, сохранив при этом уникальный деревенский шарм. Это – превосходное сочетание чистой природы, комфорта и непревзойденной кухни.

GREAT BRITAIN
OSEA ISLAND

An eclectic mix of architectural styles, there's something to suit all tastes on Osea Island. Separated from the British mainland by a mysterious tidal road, Osea takes in everything from cosy 17th century hamlets to romantic beach cottages and Edwardian mansions. Adorned with a rugged coast, rolling fields and with the winding tidal road protruding out of the dark waters of the Blackwater Estuary beyond, the vista is cinematic in its grandeur and will haunt your memories long after your island adventure comes to an end.

Die vielfältige Mischung der Architekturstile auf Osea Island bietet etwas für jeden Geschmack. Vom britischen Festland durch eine geheimnisvolle Gezeitenstraße getrennt, gibt es hier behagliche Dörfer aus dem 17. Jahrhundert, romantische Strand-Cottages und Herrenhäuser im edwardianischen Stil. Mit der zerklüfteten Küstenlinie, weiten Feldern und der Gezeitenstraße, die sich aus dem dunklen Wasser der Blackwater-Mündung windet, finden Besucher hier eine filmähnliche Szenerie, die sie nie vergessen werden.

Mélange éclectique de styles architecturaux, Osea Island répondra aux goûts les plus divers. Séparée de l'île britannique principale par une mystérieuse route submergée, Osea abrite aussi bien des hameaux du XVIIe siècle que des cabanons de plage romantiques et des manoirs édouardiens. Dotée d'une côte accidentée, de champs vallonnés et d'une route d'accès qui se découvre à marée basse dans les eaux sombres de l'estuaire de Blackwater, l'île jouit d'un panorama grandiose qui gantera vos souvenirs bien après le terme de votre aventure.

Остров Осея отличается эклектичным смешением архитектурных стилей и разнообразием. Остров отделен от британского материка таинственной дорогой приливов. Здесь есть все, от уютных деревушек 17-го века до романтических пляжных коттеджей и особняков эпохи короля Эдуарда. Пейзаж с суровым берегом, холмистыми полями и извилистой приливной дорогой, выдающейся из темных вод дельты Блэкуотер, кинемотографичен в своем величии и надолго сохранится у вас в памяти.

GREAT BRITAIN
SPITBANK FORT

Forming part of the Portsmouth's Solent Strait, Spitbank Fort is perhaps the only private island in Britain to be protected by six-metre-thick walls. Recently converted from a former military defence to a luxury hotel, Spitbank Fort promises a private island experience never to forget. Decadently decorated to make the most of their historic charm, each of Spitbank's nine bedrooms has a different story to tell. Offering all the pomp of the old Empire, this incredible destination will provide guests with something to talk about for years to come.

Spitbank Fort gehört zu Portsmouths Solent Strait und ist wohl die einzige Privatinsel Englands, die von sechs Meter dicken Mauern geschützt wird. Von einem Militärstützpunkt in ein Luxushotel verwandelt, verspricht Spitbank Fort Abenteuer, die man nie vergessen wird. Verschwenderisch im Sinne des historischen Charmes dekoriert, hat jedes der neun Schlafzimmer eine andere Geschichte zu erzählen. Die Insel hat Prunk und Pracht des Alten Reiches bewahrt und ihre Besucher werden noch Jahre davon erzählen können.

Spitbank Fort fait partie du détroit de Solen de Portsmouth et constitue probablement la seule île privée britannique protégée par des murs de six mètres d'épaisseur. Récemment reconverti en un hôtel de luxe, l'ancien fort vous promet une aventure inoubliable. Somptueusement décorées pour mettre en valeur leur charme historique, les neuf chambres ont chacune un récit à vous raconter. Avec tout le faste du vieil Empire, cette incroyable destination offrira à ses invités un sujet de conversation pour les années à venir.

Являясь частью пролива Солент в Портсмуте, Форт Спитбанк – это, пожалуй, единственный частный остров в Великобритании, который защищен стенами толщиной 6 метров. Недавно переоборудованный из бывшего военного укрепления в роскошный отель, Форт Спитбанк стал превосходным местом для отдыха на частном острове. Роскошное оформление подчеркивает исторический шарм отеля, где каждая из девяти спальней имеет свою историю. В этом невероятном месте собрано все великолепие старой империи, и гостям, несомненно, будет о чем поговорить на многие годы.

SWEDEN
STORA RULLINGEN

Take advantage of the long Scandinavian summer days and improve your handicap on this former Viking stronghold in Sweden. Overlooking the breathtaking Lake Mälaren and located only one hour away from Stockholm, Stora Rullingen boasts a private and secluded four-bedroom family home decorated in typical Scandinavian style, as well as a hunting lodge, stables and six tee-off points, which combine to form an unstructured golf course. This pearl of a private island is the perfect place to get back in to the swing of things.

Auf Schwedens einstigem Wikinger-Stützpunkt genießt man die langen skandinavischen Sommernächte und verbessert sein Golf-Handicap. Stora Rollingen ist nur eine Stunde von Stockholm entfernt und blickt auf den herrlichen Mälarsee. Die Privatinsel bietet ein abgeschiedenes, intimes Familienheim mit vier Schlafzimmern im typisch skandinavischen Stil sowie eine Jagdhütte, Ställe und einen Golfplatz mit sechs Abschlagpunkten. Eine seltene Perle, die Besuchern nicht nur beim Golf neuen Schwung verleiht.

Profitez des longues journées d'été de la Scandinavie pour réduire votre handicap dans cette ancienne forteresse viking, en Suède. Surplombant l'impressionnant lac de Mälaren, à une heure de Stockholm, Stora Rullingen abrite une maison de famille reculée de quatre chambres, dans un style typique. Vous trouverez également une cabane de chasseur, des écuries et un parcours de golf libre de six trous. Cette perle est l'endroit idéal pour redéfinir son approche des choses.

Воспользуйтесь длинными скандинавскими летними днями и побывайте в бывшей крепости викингов в Швеции. Остров Стора Руллинген с великолепным видом на озеро Меларен находится всего в часе езды от Стокгольма. Здесь есть частный уединенный дом с четырьмя спальнями, оформленными в традиционном скандинавском стиле, а также охотничий домик, конюшни и нестандартное поле для гольфа. Эта жемчужина частных островов — идеальное место, где можно отдохнуть, забыв о делах.

SWEDEN
ISLAND LODGE BERGHOLMEN

For the best eco-experience in Scandinavia, look no further than the Island Lodge Bergholmen. Combining rugged landscapes and chic Scandinavian design, this is a camping experience unlike any other. Made up of seven high-tech twin-bed tents, the island is perfect for small groups and corporate events – providing a tranquil environment filled with plenty of adventure. Our top tip? Jump in the 40°C wood-fired tub and bask in bubbling waters with a cool beer and even cooler views of the Stockholm Archipelago beyond.

Das beste Öko-Erlebnis Skandinaviens bietet die Island Lodge auf Bergholmen. Die zerklüftete Landschaft und das schicke skandinavische Design sorgen für eine völlig neue Camping-Erfahrung. Mit sieben High-Tech-Doppelzelten ist diese Insel ideal für kleine Gruppen und Business Events. Die Umgebung ist ruhig und verspricht dennoch Abenteuer. Unser Geheimtipp? Ein sprudelndes Bad im 40° C warmen, vom Holzfeuer erhitzten Wasser mit einem kühlen Bier vor dem Panorama des Stockholmer Schärengartens.

Vous recherchez la meilleure des éco-expériences en Scandinavie ? N'allez pas plus loin que l'Island Lodge Bergholmen. Mêlant paysages rugueux et élégance nordique, cet espace de camping est sans pareil. Dotée de sept tentes high-tech à lits doubles, l'île peut idéalement accueillir de petits groupes et des événements d'entreprise, dans un environnement calme où l'aventure est reine. Notre conseil ? Sautez dans le jacuzzi à 40° chauffé au bois et détendez-vous dans les eaux bouillonnantes en buvant une bière fraîche, avec vue sur l'archipel de Stockholm.

Для идеального отдыха в экологически чистом месте в Скандинавии достаточно посетить остров Бергхолмен. Суровый ландшафт в сочетании с шикарным скандинавским дизайном сделают такой отдых на природе незабываемым. Семь палаток с двуспальными кроватями созданы с использованием самых современных технологий. Этот остров идеально подходит для небольших групп и проведения корпоративных мероприятий. Здесь гостей ждет спокойная обстановка и множество приключений. Хотите совет? Прыгайте в разогретую на огне дровяную ванну с пузырьками и наслаждайтесь прохладным пивом и замечательными видами Стокгольмского архипелага.

L'HÔTEL SPA DES PÊCHEURS – ÎLE DE CAVALLO
FRANCE

An exclusive paradise with everything close to hand, l'Île de Cavallo is found in one of the most picturesque corners of southern Europe, just off the coast of Corsica. Comprised of beautiful beaches, rugged coasts and Mediterranean flair, Cavallo forms the perfect place to sit back and unwind. Famed for its all-encompassing spa treatments, the island is perfect for impulsive indulgence and romantic weekend breaks. For an extra special treat, check yourself into The Suite – a luxurious residence set atop a rugged, rocky inlet.

Ein exklusives Paradies, in dem es an nichts mangelt. Die Île de Cavallo liegt direkt vor Korsikas Küste, in einer der schönsten Ecken Südeuropas. Die Mischung aus herrlichen Stränden, zerklüfteten Küsten und mediterranem Flair macht Cavallo zum perfekten Erholungs- und Entspannungsort. Berühmt für ihre ganzheitlichen Spa-Behandlungen ist die Insel ideal für ein spontanes Verwöhnprogramm und romantische Wochenenden. Ein besonderes Highlight ist die Suite – eine Luxusresidenz auf zerklüfteten Felsen.

Ce paradis exclusif a tout à portée de main. L'Île de Cavallo se trouve dans l'une des régions les plus spectaculaires d'Europe du sud, au large de la Corse. Avec ses plages magnifiques, ses côtes accidentées et son élégance méditerranéenne, Cavallo est le lieu idéal pour se poser et se détendre. Réputée pour son spa et ses soins exhaustifs, l'île s'accorde parfaitement avec vos envies d'escapade romantique d'un week-end. Faites-vous un petit plaisir supplémentaire et venez découvrir La Suite, une résidence de luxe juchée au sommet d'un îlot rocailleux.

Остров Кавалло – это эксклюзивный райский уголок, где все находится под рукой. Он расположен в одном из самых живописных уголков южной Европы, недалеко от побережья Корсики. Прекрасные пляжи, скалистые берега и средиземноморское обаяние делают Кавалло идеальным местом, где можно отдохнуть и расслабиться. Остров знаменит своими уникальными спа-процедурами. Это совершенное место для сиюминутных наслаждений и романтических выходных. А чтобы воспользоваться дополнительными преимуществами и особым обращением, забронируйте The Suite – роскошную резиденцию, расположенную в бухте на самой вершине скалы.

L'ÎLE À BOIS
FRANCE

With its spectacular landscapes and breath-taking views of the Breton coastline, l'île à Bois is a truly unforgettable island holiday destination with space for up to 15 guests. Combining ever-changing sky-scapes and rugged coastlines, the marvellous scenery and changing light of this region is said to have inspired a whole host of famous artists, including the likes of as Paul Signac, Maximilien Luce, Henri Rivière and even Matisse. This 15 hectare Breton beauty is sure to leave a lasting impression.

Spektakuläre Landschaften und die Sicht auf die bretonische Küste machen die l'île à Bois zu einem unvergesslichen Urlaubsziel für bis zu 15 Gäste. Die ewig wechselnden Farben des Himmels, die raue Küstenlinie und herrliche Landschaft mit ihren Lichtspielen sollen schon viele berühmte Künstler inspiriert haben, darunter Paul Signac, Maximilien Luce, Henri Rivière und sogar Matisse. 15 Hektar bretonische Schönheit hinterlassen einen bleibenden Eindruck.

Avec ses paysages spectaculaires et la vue époustouflante sur les côtes bretonnes, l'Île à Bois est une destination inoubliable capable d'accueillir jusqu'à 15 invités. Son ciel mouvant et ses rivages accidentés, ses panoramas féeriques et ses jeux de lumière ont inspiré nombre d'artistes connus, tels que Paul Signac, Maximilien Luce, Henri Rivière et même Matisse. Cette perle bretonne de 15 hectares laissera une marque indélébile sur votre imagination.

Остров Иль-а-Буа со своими эффектными ландшафтами и захватывающими видами бретонского побережья является поистине незабываемым местом для отпуска и может принять до 15 гостей. Постоянно меняющиеся виды неба и суровых береговых пейзажей с их чудесной переменой освещения вдохновляли многих известных художников, таких как Поль Синьяк, Максимилиан Люс, Анри Ривьер и даже Матисс. Эта бретонская красота на площади 15 гектаров, несомненно, оставит у вас неизгладимое впечатление.

ÎLE DE CHANTEMESLE FRANCE

Looking like something from an impressionist masterpiece, it will come as little surprise to culture vultures that the quaint countryside surrounding l'Île de Chantemesle formed the inspiration for many of France's most iconic painters. Indeed, Claude Monet lived in nearby Vétheuil, completing several important masterpieces there. Spread across 25 acres and with two charming villas built in the local style to accommodate eleven travellers, who knows how your private island holiday could inspire you?

Die Landschaft ähnelt einem impressionistischen Meisterwerk, und so wird es Kenner kaum überraschen, dass die malerische Szenerie rund um die Île de Chantemesle vielen der bekanntesten Maler Frankreichs als Inspiration gedient hat. Claude Monet hat ganz in der Nähe, in Vétheuil, gelebt und dort viele seiner Meisterwerke vollendet. Wer weiß, wozu diese zehn Hektar große Privatinsel und ihre zwei charmanten Villen, die im Stil der Region erbaut sind, ihre heutigen Besucher inspirieren mögen?

Directement sortie d'un chef-d'œuvre expressionniste, les passionnés de culture ne seront pas surpris d'apprendre que la campagne pittoresque qui entoure l'Île de Chantemesle inspira de nombreux peintres français célèbres, parmi lesquels Claude Monet, qui vécut près de Vétheuil, où il réalisa plusieurs de ses plus belles toiles. Sur près de dix hectares, deux charmantes villas peuvent accueillir onze voyageurs. Qui sait ce qu'un séjour sur cette île privée pourra vous inspirer ?

Неудивительно, что любителям культуры причудливая деревенская окрестность Иль-де-Шантимэль напоминает работы художников-импрессионистов. Этот остров вдохновил многих известных художников Франции. Более того, Клод Моне жил в соседнем городе Ветей и завершил там несколько важных работ. На площади в 25 акров расположены две очаровательные виллы в местном стиле, где могут разместиться 11 человек. Кто знает, на что вас вдохновит такой отдых на частном острове?

SPAIN
TAGOMAGO

This indulgent island couldn't be further removed from the ubiquitous Balearic beats of the Ibizan mainland. Free from the mass-tourism of San Antonio and Ibiza Town, the exclusive private island of Tagomago is the perfect place for anyone who wants to wind down and get away from it all. Boasting five sumptuous suites, an impressive sauna, an expansive pool and plenty of shelter from the prying eyes of the press, it's no wonder that celebrities the world over are queuing up to call this island their own summer retreat.

Diese dem Genuss gewidmete Insel ist Welten entfernt von den allgegenwärtigen Balearic Beats Ibizas. Frei vom Massentourismus in San Antonio und Ibiza-Stadt, ist die exklusive Privatinsel Tagomago der perfekte Ort für jeden, der Erholung fernab vom täglichen Trubel sucht. Mit fünf prächtigen Suiten, einer beeindruckenden Sauna, einem großzügigen Pool und Schutz vor den Linsen der Fotografen ist es nicht verwunderlich, dass Prominente aus aller Welt Schlange stehen, um auf dieser Insel den Sommer zu verbringen.

Cette île somptueuse ne pourrait être plus éloignée des rythmes omniprésents de l'île principale d'Ibiza dans les Baléares. Protégée du tourisme de masse de San Antonio et d'Ibiza Town, l'île privée de Tagomago est le lieu idéal pour quiconque cherche détente et tranquillité. Avec ses cinq merveilleuses suites, un sauna impressionnant, une vaste piscine et toute l'intimité nécessaire pour échapper aux regards indiscrets de la presse, il n'est pas étonnant que les célébrités du monde entier fassent la queue pour s'accaparer ce sanctuaire estival.

Этот чудесный остров далек от вездесущих балеарских ритмов острова Ибица. На эксклюзивном частном острове Тагомаго отсутствует массовый туризм таких мест, как Сан-Антонио или Ибица. Это идеальное место для того, чтобы расслабиться и скрыться от суеты. Здесь имеется пять роскошных апартаментов, великолепная сауна, просторный бассейн и возможность укрыться от вездесущей прессы. Не удивительно, что знаменитости со всего мира борются за право провести летний отдых на этом уединенном острове.

GREECE
SILVER ISLAND YOGA

Comprising only of whitewashed and blue shuttered traditional Greek homes, a church and lighthouse, Silver Island is an enchanting escape where modern distractions become a distant memory. Offering a series of delightful dawn and sunset yoga classes, this relaxing twelve person retreat promises sublime tranquility to all those in search of a sense of inner peace – a space in which to unwind and merge with nature and self. Mediterranean-inspired vegetarian cuisine and divine detoxification treatments round off this holistic haven.

Strahlend weiße Häuser mit blauen Fenster-läden im griechischen Stil, eine Kirche und ein Leuchtturm ... Silver Island ist ein zauberhafter Ort, an dem der moderne Alltag zu einer fernen Erinnerung verblasst. Das Yoga Retreat für zwölf Personen bietet herrliche Sonnen-aufgangs- und Sonnenuntergangskurse und verheißt vollkommene Gelassenheit für alle auf der Suche nach innerem Frieden. Einfach loslassen und zur Natur und zu sich selbst zurückfinden. Mediterran-inspirierte, vegetarische Küche und Entgiftungstherapien perfektionieren das holistische Paradies.

Avec ses maisons grecques traditionnelles blanches et bleues aux volets fermés, son église et son phare, Silver Island est une destination de rêve où les distractions modernes ne sont rapidement plus que de vieux souvenirs. Cette retraite pour douze personnes offre une série de cours de yoga à l'aube et au coucher du soleil. La garantie d'une sublime tranquillité pour qui cherche la paix intérieure ; un espace de détente et de communion avec la nature. La cuisine végétarienne méditerranéenne et les traitements de détoxification viendront compléter ce tableau holistique.

Состоящий лишь из белостенных традици-онных греческих домов с синими ставнями, церкви и маяка, Серебряный остров – это очаровательное место для отдыха, где можно разместить до 12 человек. Суета здесь уходит на задний план, а на рассвете и закате предлагаются восхитительные занятия йогой. Это место, где можно обрести внутренний покой, расслабиться, слиться с природой и познать свою истинную сущность. Вегетарианская кухня в средиземноморском стиле и превосход-ные очищающие процедуры прекрасно дополняют это путешествие к истокам.

SWITZERLAND
HOTEL VILLA HONEGG
"ALMOST AN ISLAND..."

An island of tranquillity built on the slopes of the imposing Bürgenstock Mountain; the Hotel Villa Honegg is truly one of a kind. Located on the fringes of Lucerne, this inspiring property offers unencumbered and uninhibited indulgence amongst the most spectacular surroundings. As opulent as it is exclusive, there can't be many better vantage points over the lake below than Honegg's incredible infinity pool, stretching stupendously along the perimeter of this awe-inspiring escape.

Eine vollkommene Oase der Ruhe, gebaut in die Hänge des imposanten Bürgenstocks. Hotel Villa Honegg ist einzigartig. Am Rande Luzerns gelegen, bietet das inspirierende Anwesen uneingeschränkten Genuss inmitten spektakulärer Umgebung. Ebenso opulent wie exklusiv gibt es wohl kaum bessere Aussichtpunkte auf den im Tal liegenden See als Honeggs unglaublichen Infinity Pool, der sich entlang des formidablen Hotels erstreckt.

Ce havre de tranquillité, construit sur les pentes de l'imposante montagne de Bürgenstock est sans pareil. L'Hôtel Villa Honegg, qui borde Lucerne, offre un luxe libre et désinhibé dans le plus spectaculaire des environnements. Aussi somptueux que protégé, le point de vue sur le lac depuis la piscine à débordement d'Honegg qui encercle ce lieu impressionnant est à couper le souffle.

Уникальный Hotel Villa Honegg — это тихий оазис, построенный на склонах величественной горы Бюргеншток в окрестностях Люцерна. В этом роскошном и эксклюзивном отеле созданы все условия для легкого и беззаботного времяпрепровождения среди изумительных окрестностей. Из расположенного по периметру переливного бассейна открываются самые красивые виды на лежащее внизу озеро.

ISLAND-HOPPING IN STYLE

Ready to depart on your own island adventure? Join the jet-set with your own private aeroplane. Ensuring that even the most remote islands are never out of reach, the Dornier Seastar is the only way to travel, linking land and ocean via the skies. Gliding effortlessly from island to island from the comfort of your cabin, this first-class amphibious aircraft is the very essence of island-hopping. With space for twelve castaways, you're certain to start your vacation in style with the Dornier Seastar.

Bereit für ein eigenes Insel-Abenteuer? Mit diesem Privatflugzeug gehört man zum Jetset. Selbst die entlegensten Inseln sind mit dem Dornier Seastar stets in Reichweite – ein elegantes Transportmittel, das den Himmel nutzt, um Ozean und Land zu verbinden. In der komfortablen Kabine gleitet man mühelos von Insel zu Insel. Dieses erstklassige Amphibienflugzeug ist der Schlüssel zum wahren Insel-Hopping. Zwölf Reisende finden darin Platz und Sie können sicher sein, dass Ihr Urlaub stilvoll beginnt.

Prêt pour une aventure sur les îles ? Rejoignez la jet-set dans votre avion privé. Les paradis les plus reculés ne sont plus qu'à quelques heures de vol. Reliez terre et mer par le ciel grâce à Dornier Seastar, le meilleur moyen de voyager. Glissez d'île en île, confortablement installé dans la cabine de cet appareil amphibie de première classe. Capable d'embarquer douze passagers, il vous garantit style et élégance.

Вы готовы отправиться в приключение на острова? Присоединяйтесь к богачам и знаменитостям и отправляйтесь в путешествие на своем собственном частном самолете. Dornier Seastar – это лучший способ добраться даже на самые дальние острова. В этом самолете-амфибии высшего класса вы можете легко перемещаться с острова на остров, не покидая своей каюты. Начните с шиком свой отпуск на борту Dornier Seastar, заняв одно из 12 комфортных пассажирских мест.

ISLAND INDEX

	Location	Region	Exclusive Island Rental	Island Resort	Self-Catering Service on Request	Robinson Island	Approx. Guest Capacity	Page No.
&Beyond Mnemba Island Lodge	Tanzania	Africa & Indian Ocean	x	x			20	176
Angsana Ihuru	Maldives	Africa & Indian Ocean	x	x			100	139
Ariara Island	Philippines	Asia, Australia & New Zealand		x			18	122
Banyan Tree Maldives Madivaru	Maldives	Africa & Indian Ocean	x	x			12	140
Bedarra Island Villa	Australia	Asia, Australia & New Zealand		x			8	108
Bird Island Lodge	Seychelles	Africa & Indian Ocean		x			50 +	139
Bonefish Cay	Bahamas	South America, Central America & The Caribbean	x				14	18
Calivigny Island	Grenada	South America, Central America & The Caribbean	x	x			50 +	42
Canouan Island	Grenadines	South America, Central America & The Caribbean		x			50 +	40
Cayo Espanto	Belize	South America, Central America & The Caribbean	x	x			18	44
Cherry Island	USA – New York	North America	x		x		28	51
Coco Privé Kuda Hithi Island	Maldives	Africa & Indian Ocean	x				12	144
Cocoa Island by COMO	Maldives	Africa & Indian Ocean		x			50 +	142
Constance Tsarabanjina Madagascar	Madagascar	Africa & Indian Ocean		x			50	174
Costaérès	France	Europe	x		x		10	181
Cousine Island	Seychelles	Africa & Indian Ocean	x	x			10 +	166
Dämmans Fyr	Norway	Europe	x		x		24	181
DEDON Island Resort	Philippines	Asia, Australia & New Zealand		x			30	116
Denis Island	Seychelles	Africa & Indian Ocean		x			50 +	139
Desroches Island Resort	Seychelles	Africa & Indian Ocean		x			50 +	170
East Brother Island	USA – California	North America			x		10	58
Fafa Island Resort	Tonga	South Pacific	x	x			30	82
Forsyth Island	New Zealand	Asia, Australia & New Zealand	x		x		6 (+ 4)	100
Fota Island	Ireland	Europe		x			50 +	181
Frégate Island Private	Seychelles	Africa & Indian Ocean	x	x			40	156
Galloo Island	USA – New York	North America	x		x		12	56
Gili Lankanfushi	Maldives	Africa & Indian Ocean		x			100 +	139
Guana Island	British Virgin Islands	South America, Central America & The Caribbean	x	x			32	26
Heron Island	Australia	Asia, Australia & New Zealand		x			100 +	110
Hotel Villa Honegg	Switzerland	Europe		x			50 +	210
Hunt Island	Canada – Nova Scotia	North America	x		x		6	62
Île de Chantemesle	France	Europe	x		x		11	202
Île des Deux Cocos	Mauritius	Africa & Indian Ocean	x	x			5	172
Isla de Coco	Panama	South America, Central America & The Caribbean	x			x	10	9
Isla Robinson Crusoe	Chile	South America, Central America & The Caribbean				x	20 +	9
Island Hideaway at Dhonakulhi	Maldives	Africa & Indian Ocean		x			100 +	148
Island Lodge Bergholmen	Sweden	Europe	x	x			14	196
Isle of Eriska	Scotland	Europe	x	x			50 +	184
King Pacific Lodge	Canada – British Columbia	North America		x			50	51
Kura Kura Resort and Krakal Island	Indonesia	Asia, Australia & New Zealand		x		x	70 +	132
L'île à Bois	France	Europe	x		x		15	200
L'Hôtel Spa des Pêcheurs - Île de Cavallo	France	Europe		x			100 +	198
Laucala Island	Fiji	South Pacific	x	x			50	68
Lissenung Island Resort	Papua New Guinea	South Pacific		x			10	67
Little Whale Cay	Bahamas	South America, Central America & The Caribbean	x				12	14
Lizard Island	Australia	Asia, Australia & New Zealand		x			50 +	99
Løksøya Island	Norway	Europe	x		x		5	181
Lomani Island	Fiji	South Pacific	x	x			50 +	67
Makepeace Island	Australia	Asia, Australia & New Zealand	x	x			22	112
Melody Key	USA - Florida	North America	x		x		10	60

	Location	Region	Exclusive Island Rental	Island Resort	Self-Catering Service on Request	Robinson Island	Approx. Guest Capacity	Page No.
Mersey River Lodge	Canada – Nova Scotia	North America	x		x		10	51
Mirihi Island Resort	Maldives	Africa & Indian Ocean		x			72	150
Motu Tané	French Polynesia	South Pacific	x	x			20	67
Motu Teta	French Polynesia	South Pacific	x	x			10	67
Mounu Island	Tonga	South Pacific	x	x			6	67
Musha Cay	Bahamas	South America, Central America & The Caribbean	x	x			24	10
Mustique Island	Grenadines	South America, Central America & The Caribbean		x			100 +	34
Naladhu Maldives	Maldives	Africa & Indian Ocean		x			50	139
Namale Resort & Spa	Fiji	South Pacific		x			30	72
Nautilus Island	USA – Maine	North America	x		x		8	51
Necker Island	British Virgin Islands	South America, Central America & The Caribbean	x	x			28	28
Nikoi Island	Indonesia	Asia, Australia & New Zealand	x	x			50	134
North Island	Seychelles	Africa & Indian Ocean	x	x			22 +	160
One&Only Reethi Rah	Maldives	Africa & Indian Ocean		x			100 +	152
Osea Island	Great Britain	Europe	x	x			50 +	188
Over Yonder Cay	Bahamas	South America, Central America & The Caribbean	x				28	20
Pangkor Laut Resort	Malaysia	Asia, Australia & New Zealand		x			50 +	128
Parrot Cay by COMO	Turks and Caicos	South America, Central America & The Caribbean		x			100 +	22
Peter Island Resort & Spa	British Virgin Islands	South America, Central America & The Caribbean	x	x			100 +	32
Petit St. Vincent	Grenadines	South America, Central America & The Caribbean		x			50	38
Pohuenui Island	New Zealand	Asia, Australia & New Zealand	x		x		15	106
Porcada	Panama	South America, Central America & The Caribbean	x		x		10	46
Private Island Bora Bora	French Polynesia	South Pacific	x	x			50	86
Pulau Joyo	Indonesia	Asia, Australia & New Zealand		x			30	136
Pumpkin Island	Australia	Asia, Australia & New Zealand	x	x			30	99
Ratua Private Island	Vanuatu	South Pacific		x			30	92
Royal Belize	Belize	South America, Central America & The Caribbean	x	x			10	9
Royal Davui Island Resort	Fiji	South Pacific	x	x			30	74
Sanda Island	Scotland	Europe	x	x			10 +	186
Silver Island Yoga	Greece	Europe	x	x			12	206
Singer Castle on Dark Island	USA - New York	North America	x		x		4	52
Soneva Fushi	Maldives	Africa & Indian Ocean	x	x			100 +	154
Soneva Kiri Resort	Thailand	Asia, Australia & New Zealand	x	x			50 +	99
Song Saa Private Island	Cambodia	Asia, Australia & New Zealand	x	x			50 +	124
Spitbank Fort	Great Britain	Europe	x	x			20	190
Stora Rullingen	Sweden	Europe	x	x			10	194
Tagomago	Spain	Europe	x	x			10	204
Taprobane Island	Sri Lanka	Asia, Australia & New Zealand	x	x			8	130
Tavanipupu	Solomon Islands	South Pacific	x	x			32	94
The Beach House at Iruveli	Maldives	Africa & Indian Ocean	x	x			50 +	139
The Naka Island	Thailand	Asia, Australia & New Zealand	x	x			50 +	114
The Wakaya Club & Spa	Fiji	South Pacific	x	x			28	80
Toberua Island Resort	Fiji	South Pacific	x	x			30	76
Tresco Island	Great Britain	Europe		x			50 +	181
Turtle Island	Fiji	South Pacific	x	x			28	67
Vahine Island Resort	French Polynesia	South Pacific	x	x			10	90
Vamizi Island	Mozambique	Africa & Indian Ocean	x	x			30	178
Vatulele Island Resort	Fiji	South Pacific	x	x			50	66
Wadigi Island Resort Fiji	Fiji	South Pacific	x					78
Waterford Castle Hotel & Golf Resort	Ireland	Europe	x	x			50 +	182
Wilson Island	Australia	Asia, Australia & New Zealand	x	x			12	99

Musha Cay, Bahamas

PHOTO CREDITS

Cover photo: (Little Whale Cay) courtesy of Little Whale Cay
Back cover photos: top left (Musha Cay) courtesy of Musha Cay,
        top right (Laucala Island) courtesy of Laucala Island,
        bottom left (Angsana Ihuru) courtesy of Angsana Ihuru,
        bottom right (Singer Castle) by Farhad Vladi

p. 03 by Jakob Studnar
p. 07 by Kwintowski Photography
p. 09 (Isla Robinson Crusoe) by Chile Tourism,
    (Isla de Coco) by Farhad Vladi, (Royal Belize) by HIT Photograhy
p. 10 (Musha Cay) by Farhad Vladi
pp. 12-13 (Musha Cay) courtesy of Musha Cay
pp. 14-17 (Little Whale Cay) by Dan Einzig/delicious-photo.co.uk,
        p. 16 bottom courtesy of Little Whale Cay
pp. 18-19 (Bonefish Cay) courtesy of Bonefish Cay, p. 19 top by John D. Slack
pp. 20-21 (Over Yonder Cay) by Dana Jinkins, Duncan Hipkin, Rodney Waters
pp. 22-25 (Parrot Cay by Como) courtesy of COMO Hotels and Resorts,
        p. 24 by Donna Karan's Sanctuary
pp. 26-27 (Guana Island) by Rainbow Visions, courtesy of Guana Island
        p. 27 bottom left by Design Lounge, courtesy of Guana Island
pp. 28-31 (Necker Island) courtesy of Necker Island
pp. 32-33 (Peter Island Resort & Spa) courtesy of Peter Island Resort & Spa
pp. 34-37 (Mustique Island) courtesy of Mustique Company
pp. 38-39 (Petit St. Vincent) by Jonathan Palmer,
        p. 39 by Mike Toy Photography
pp. 40-41 (Canouan Island) courtesy of Canouan Island
pp. 42-43 (Calivigny Island) by Kwintowski Photography
pp. 44-45 (Cayo Espanto) courtesy of Cayo Espanto
pp. 46-49 (Porcada) by Christian Schriefer, p. 47 bottom right by Farhad Vladi
pp. 51 (Nautilus Island) by Ben Magro, (Mersey River Lodge) by Farhad Vladi,
    (King Pacific Lodge) courtesy of King Pacific Lodge,
    (Cherry Island) by James Scherzi
pp. 52-55 (Singer Castle) by Ian Coristine, 1000 Islands Photo Art,
        pp. 54-55 by Farhad Vladi
pp. 56-57 (Galloo Island) by Farhad Vladi
pp. 58-59 (East Brother Island) by Farhad Vladi,
        p. 59 right courtesy of East Brother Light Station, Inc.
pp. 60-61 (Melody Key) courtesy of Melody Key Private Island
pp. 62-65 (Hunt Island) by David Burns, p. 64 by Farhad Vladi
p. 66 (Vatulele Island Resort) courtesy of Vatulele Island Resort
p. 67 (Turtle Island) by James Walshe, (Lomani Island) by Peter Henning
    (Mounu Island) by Mounu David Kingsland,
    (Lissenung Island Resort) courtesy of Lissenung Island Resort,
    (Motu Tané) courtesy of Motu Tané,
    (Motu Teta) courtesy of Motu Teta Private Island
pp. 68-71 (Laucala Island) courtesy of Laucala Island
pp. 72-73 (Namale Resort & Spa) courtesy of Namale Resort & Spa
pp. 74-75 (Royal Davui Island Resort) courtesy of Royal Davui Island Resort
pp. 76-77 (Toberua Island Resort) courtesy of Toberua Island Resort
pp. 78-79 (Wadigi Island) courtesy of Wadigi Island
pp. 80-81 (The Wakaya Club & Spa) courtesy of The Wakaya Club & Spa,
        p. 81 bottom Helmut Koller
pp. 82-85 (Fafa Island Resort) by Franc Marc Frei
pp. 86-89 (Private Island Bora Bora) by Grégoire le Bacon
        p. 87 top by Philippe Bacchet
pp. 90-91 (Vahine Island Resort) by Eric Pinel,
        p. 90 top and middle courtesy of Vahine Island
pp. 92-93 (Ratua Private Island) courtesy of Ratua Island
pp. 94-97 (Tavanipupu Private Island) courtesy of Tavanipupu Private Island
pp. 99 (Pumpkin Island) by Adam Gormley,
    (Wilson Island) courtesy of Wilson Island,
    (Lizard Island) courtesy of Lizard Island,
    (Soneva Kiri Resort) by Herbert Ypma
pp. 100-105 (Forsyth Island) by David Burns
pp. 106-107 (Pohuenui Island) by Farhad Vladi,
        p. 107 courtesy of Pohuenui Island

pp. 108-109 (Bedarra Island) by Prue Roscoe, courtesy of Contemporary
        Hotels, p. 108 top courtesy of Bedarra Island
pp. 110-111 (Heron Island) courtesy of Heron Island
pp. 112-113 (Makepeace Island) courtesy of Makepeace Island
pp. 114-115 (Naka Island) courtesy of Naka Island
pp. 116-121 (Dedon Island Resort) by Paul Barbera
pp. 122-123 (Ariara Island) by Al Linsangan
pp. 124-127 (Song Saa Private Island) by Markus Gortz
pp. 128-129 (Pangkor Laut Resort) courtesy of Pangkor Laut Resort
pp. 130-131 (Taprobane Island) courtesy of Taprobane Island
pp. 132-133 (Kura Kura Resort & Krakal Island) courtesy of Kura Kura Resort
pp. 134-135 (Nikoi Island) courtesy of Nikoi Island
pp. 136-137 (Pulau Joyo) courtesy of Pulau Joyo
p. 139 (Naladhu Maldives) courtesy of Naladhu Maldives,
    (Angsana Ihuru) courtesy of Angsana Ihuru,
    (Gili Lankanfushi) courtesy of Gili Lankanfushi,
    (Beach House Iruveli) courtesy of Beach House Iruveli/
    Beach House Collection,
    (Bird Island Lodge) by Gregor Kervina,
    (Denis Island) courtesy of Denis Island
pp. 140-141 (Banyan Tree Madivaru) courtesy of Banyan Tree Madivaru
pp. 142-143 (Cocoa Island By Como) courtesy of COMO Hotels and Resorts
pp. 144-147 (Coco Privé Kuda Hithi Island) courtesy of Coco Privé Kuda
        Hithi Island
pp. 148-149 (Island Hideaway at Dhonakulhi) courtesy of Island Hideaway
        at Dhonakulhi Maldives
pp. 150-151 (Mirihi Island Resort) courtesy of Mirihi Island Resort
pp. 152-153 (One&Only Reethi Rah) courtesy of One&Only Rethi Rah
pp. 154-155 (Soneva Fushi) courtesy of Soneva Fushi Resort,
        p. 155 top by Kieattipong Panchee, bottom right by Herbert Ypma
pp. 156-159 (Frégate Island Private) courtesy of Frégate Island Private
pp. 160-165 (North Island) courtesy of Wilderness Safaris
pp. 166-169 (Cousine Island) by Martin Harvey,
        p. 168, p. 169 bottom by Paul Turcotte
pp. 170-171 (Desroches Island) courtesy of Desroches Island
pp. 172-173 (Île Des Deux Cocos) courtesy of LUX* Resort
pp. 174-175 (Constance Tsarabanjina Madagascar) courtesy of
        Constance Tsarabanjina Madagascar
pp. 176-177 (&Beyond Mnemba Island Lodge) courtesy of
        &Beyond Mnemba Island Lodge
pp. 178-179 (Vamizi Island) courtesy of Vamizi Island
p. 181 (Løksøya) by David Burns, (Fota Island Resort) by Roger Overall
    courtesy of Fota Island Resort, (Dämmans Fyr) courtesy of Dämmans Fyr,
    (Costaérès) by Farhad Vladi, (Tresco Island) courtesy of Tresco Island
pp. 182-183 (Waterford Castle Hotel & Golf Resort) by Shane O'Neill
        Aspec Photography
pp. 184-185 (Isle of Eriska) courtesy of Isle Eriksa,
        p. 185 top left by Farhad Vladi
pp. 186-187 (Sanda Island) by Farhad Vladi,
        p. 187 middle and top courtesy of Sanda Island
pp. 188-189 (Osea Island) courtesy of Osea Island
pp. 190-193 (Spitbank Fort) by Pete Canning courtesy of Solent Forts
pp. 194-195 (Stora Rullingen) courtesy of Stora Rullingen
pp. 196-197 (Island Lodge Berghomen) by Torkild Berglund
pp. 198-199 (L'Hôtel Spa des Pêcheurs – Île de Cavallo) courtesy of
        L'Hôtel Spa des Pêcheurs
pp. 200-201 (L'Île à Bois) by Catherine Gaillemain, bottom by John LeFevre
pp. 202-203 (Île de Chantemesle) courtesy of Île de Chantemesle
pp. 204-205 (Tagomago) by Matthias Kühn courtesy of Tagomago
pp. 206-209 (Silver Island Yoga) by Lissa & Claire Christie
pp. 210-213 (Hotel Villa Honegg) by Timo Schwach courtesy of
        Hotel Villa Honegg
pp. 214-215 (Island-Hopping in Style) courtesy of Dornier Seawings
p. 218 (Musha Cay) courtesy of Musha Cay

Bahamas » Little Whale Cay

IMPRINT & BOOKING CONTACT

For expert advice on booking your very own *Cool Private Island Resort* vacation, contact *Vladi Private Islands Travel*, the world's first travel agency dedicated exclusively to private island rental. Whether you're planning a private island wedding, a wicked weekend-break, an island-hopping adventure or simply the holiday of a lifetime, *Vladi Private Islands Travel* is your ticket to private island luxury. For further details about all of our 101 Cool Private Island Resorts or to view the rest of our extensive island collection, visit www.private-islands.com

Booking contact:

VLADI PRIVATE ISLANDS
Ballindamm 7
20095 Hamburg
Germany

Tel.: +49 40 33 00 00
Fax.: +49 40 33 00 81
E-mail: travel@private-islands.com

VLADI PRIVATE ISLANDS
Suite 602, Summit Place
1601 Lower Water Street
Halifax, Nova Scotia B3J 3P6
Canada

Tel.: +1 902 423 3202
Fax: +1 902 425 4765
E-mail: travel@private-islands.com

MIX
Papier aus verantwortungsvollen Quellen
Paper from responsible sources
FSC® C005833

Published by teNeues Publishing Group
teNeues Verlag GmbH + Co. KG
Am Selder 37, 47906 Kempen, Germany
Phone: +49 (0)2152 916 0, Fax: +49 (0)2152 916 111
e-mail: books@teneues.de

Press Department: Andrea Rehn
Phone: +49 (0)2152 916 202
e-mail: arehn@teneues.de

TENEUES DIGITAL MEDIA GMBH
Kohlfurter Straße 41–43, 10999 Berlin, Germany
Phone: +49 (0)30 700 77 65 0

teNeues Publishing Company
7 West 18th Street, New York, NY 10011, USA
Phone: +1 212 627 9090, Fax: +1 212 627 9511

teNeues Publishing UK Ltd.
12 Ferndene Road, London SE24 0AQ, UK
Phone: +44 (0)20 3542 8997

teNeues France S.A.R.L.
39, rue des Billets, 18250 Henrichemont, France
Phone: +33 (0)2 4826 9348, Fax: +33 (0)1 7072 3482

www.teneues.com

© 2013 teNeues Verlag GmbH + Co. KG, Kempen
ISBN: 978-3-8327-9700-3
Library of Congress Control Number: 2013930380
Printed in the Czech Republic

Edited by Farhad Vladi & Olaf Lock
Foreword by Farhad Vladi
Texts by Emma Sharples
Editorial Management by Annika Drewinat
Special thanks to Martina Matthiesen, Kai Bommersheim
& the Travel Team at Vladi Private Islands

Produced by TENEUES DIGITAL MEDIA GMBH
Publishing Director: Martin Nicholas Kunz
Editorial Coordination, Photo Editing: Heike Fademrecht, Betti Fiegle, Sabine Wabnitz, Franziska Giovannini
Translation: Kerstin Struck (de), Thomas André (fr), Karina Maria Borowiak, Steffen Beilich, Sprachwerkstatt Berlin, Yanika Cheme (ru)
Copy Editing: Kerstin Struck, Nicholas Thompson
Art Direction, Design: Christin Steirat
Layout, Prepress: Sophie Franke
Imaging: Tridix, Berlin